FEMININE FEMINIST

A Missing Link Eluding Discovery

Niccolò

Feminine Feminist: A Missing Link Eluding Discovery

by Niccolò

ISBN 978-1-64550-502-0 (paperback)

CONTENTS

This book is part of a 2019 decalogue consisting of

- Sign of Times: Music Anthology and Lyric Analysis

- Hollywood Misogyny

- Beginners' Guide to the FED:
  Why it is Unique on our Planet

- The Kennedy Kurse: Four Obvious Konnektions

- Manichaeism and Satanic Child Abuse

- Progressive Intolerance: Last Stop Before Hitler

- Patriotic Ingenuousness

- Deism versus Theism:
  2-7 in the Scientific Arena of the 20th Century

- Feminine Feminist:
  A Missing Link Eluding Discovery

- The Snake: Three Millennia of Anti-Semitism

The half-blood Mary Thompson Fisher:
the last known feminine feminist

INTRODUCTION
Missing Link

I.1 Mary Thompson Fisher:
Second and Last Feminine Feminist

Mary Thompson Fisher was born in 1895, near Emet, Oklahoma. She was daughter of a German mother and a native American Father, born in Chickasaw Nation (later reduced to a Native Reserve in Oklahoma). Mary's vocation occurred when she once assisted, a young girl, at a ritual dance of her tribe. Halfway the ritual, she felt the impulse to join the dancers and started running towards them. Her father quickly fetched her, and said her it was not allowed to tread between the dancers and the central fire — no doubt a Holy Place. A sudden burst of rain interrupted the ritual. Seeing Mary's inconsolable tears, an old man approached her, and told her something soothing in native American. Although she did not understand, her father did. He waited many years before telling her.

In Frankowski's 2016 movie "Te Ata", the story writers Mrs. Luttrell and Barbour provide some (possibly non-historic) details about Mary's life. Shortly after the interrupted traditional dance she declared to need a stage name. Her parents did all they could to fine one, knowing the somewhat obstinate character of their daughter. Finally, a name appeared that met with everybody's approval: "Te Ata", meaning "Bearer of the Morning."

In order to realize her vocation, she set her sights on Broadway. In spite of her father's explicit protests[1] (though not without his explicit consent), she left Chickasaw for an academic education. Life was quite tough for Te Ata: during her first year at university all her class mates ignored her, her two roommates included. Her humility and spirit of tacit acceptation turned the well-to-do-white-ladies like a leaf, and the second year she was generally admired. After graduating, looking for a job, she ran into so many rejections that she began to wonder whether she was really cut out for the bright lights.

---

[1] Her father loved her so much that he could not stand the feeling of his not being able to protect her

Meanwhile, she fell in love with a 17-years older German multidisciplinary scientist. His surprise knew no limits when Mary wanted him to ask her father's permission to marry her. Knowing about Mary's strength of character, and profound convictions, he did not even blink. As her father[2] could not find a single shortcoming in the German scientist,[3] Mary got it her way.

On his death bed, her father told Mary what the old man tried to tell her when the ritual dance was interrupted: to wit, that she was destined to tell all Americans about the ritual dance she had testified as a child.

In spite of her continuous failures in finding even the lowliest job, she kept insisting — always without success, until... she met Eleanor Roosevelt.

The feminist reader might think: "what could I ever learn from Mary, who was so retrograde as to ask her father's permission to leave her home town, or to marry? Such is not feminism, but the very opposite: plain submission to a patriarchal society!"

---

[2] Obviously unhappy with her marrying a stranger to the Chickasaw Nation

[3] During her whole life, her husband encouraged her, with words and deeds, in achieving her personal vocation.

Perhaps.[4]

Although one should not make the silly mistake to compare every society with ours today. Who knows, the beginning of the third millennium after Christ will once receive the etiquette "dark age of enlightened sexual slave trade and large-scale butchery of unborns". Moreover, there are so many kinds of feminism that I could not tell with certainty that all of them consider Mary's behavior submissive-patriarchal *in her culture*.

By the way, my dear feminists: in Buddhist India, the patriarchal agreement between two families concerning their children's marriage still holds today. Poor Indian marriages have a much higher survival probability than rich Western ones: *And that is definitely not because Indian women are more submissive to husbands than those in rich Western societies.*

A *young* native American girl leaving her country *alone*, obviously was unheard of in Chickasaw. She was the first native half-blood to go to university, leaving behind a much loved and heavily frustrated father.[5] This must have torn her sensible heart apart. How many

---

4   In India this is still the ordinary practice, as in nearly all
    traditional cultures, whose lack of wealth prevented the total
    degradation of sexuality to consumption.
5   Frustrated, out of love, obviously

modern feminists are willing to make such offers for reaching their ideals? In Frankowski's movie, at some occasion, Te Ata categorically refused to exchange her own native clothes for some sexy outfit offered to her, even though that meant, again, no job, and worse, no hope of telling her native stories to the whole nation. Te Ata is, in my personal view, an accomplished feminist, *without concessions concerning her femininity.*

I.2 Economy

Not being a professional economist myself, I will not confront you with complicated econometrical equations. The only economical concept used in this book, is that a higher market demand leads to higher prices, and higher market offer to lower prices.

In this pamphlet I wish to criticize a chronic omission in all known economic theories: the failure of taking into account the average mental health of a population. This does not mean I do not agree with extant well-established econometrists' equations. As a scientist I simply believe that a very large majority consensus in whatever scientific field of investigation implies scientific truth. Hence, the omission does not *invalidate* economic theories: it only *reduces their domain of validity.*[6] All econometric equations hold for both a highly moral society, and an immoral society. The only difference is that some free parameters in economic models have quite different values.

A simple example of the social costs of lack of moral health in a society, are insurance and lawyers' costs for a businessman doing a transaction. In a highly moral society, a business man does not need either off them: he simply trusts the honorability of his partner in trade. As the society becomes more and more immoral, a businessman must necessarily spend more and more money on insurance and lawyers.

The standard objection is that insurance companies and lawyers pay their income taxes just like the business man. I fully agree. *However,* in a morally healthy society *almost all members can dedicate themselves to research and development, production and export* (RDP&E). Hence, the growth potential of a moral society is orders of magnitude higher than that of an immoral society.

The same holds for the government's fight against corruption. Corruption costs the US society billions of

---

6   See my book "deism versus theism" for more details.

dollars yearly. Since fighting corruption allows no RDP&E, all money invested in that fight is thrown away. All this does not enter into economic theories, because that is exactly what EZ flourishes upon. And no doubt, all economic Nobel Prizes go to EZ-approved theories.

Apart from all immorality mentioned above, Europe is blessed with huge administrations. Consider the following example. The Dutch Ministry of Education busies itself with monthly re-inventing the wheel. High Schools are supposed to comply with every crazy guideline created on desks of incompetent officials that execute orders from even more incompetent officials. Result is that school administrations spend 90% of their time on trying to respond adequately to the constant stream of self-contradictory guidelines emitted by the Ministry of Education.

Most of those issues can easily be decided by the schools themselves: that is nothing but the Catholic Church's **principle of subsidiarity**. It is the very opposite of **the socialist principle of bureaucracy and non-productivity**.

In my view, the only three issues the Ministry of Education is responsible for, are (i) determining the content of the final high-school exams, (ii) overseeing that all schools receive enough copies of these exams *on the very day of the exam*, (iii) checking that the punctuation criteria do not differ too much from school to school, and (iv) yearly report a list of average graduations per school.

Does one need tens of thousands of coffee-addicted personnel for realizing just that? I doubt it. A simple computer program would suffice.

Pay the superfluous officials a real education, and send them home when they obtain their job. Lots of money are thus available for what an economy really needs: RDP&E.

I will not talk about the bureaucratic infantilism of Brussels and Stuttgart, for that belongs to the department of crimes against humanity.

I.3 Brain Science

Consider the following non-specialist paper written by Simon Baron-Cohen, an English medical expert in idiopathic hypogonadotrophic hypogonadism (IHH), in Androgen Insensitivity Syndrome (AIS), and in congenital adrenal hyperplasia (CAH), based in Cambridge.

The Essential Difference: the male and female brain[7]

The field of sex differences in psychology is not new, though today it enjoys greater academic freedom than in past decades. The 1960s and 70s, whilst socially liberating, also made an open-minded debate about any possible role of biology contributing to psychological sex differences impossible. Those who explored the role of biology – even whilst acknowledging the importance of culture – found themselves accused of defending an essentialism that perpetuated inequalities between the sexes, and of oppression. Not a climate in which scientists can ask questions about mechanisms in nature. Today, the pendulum has settled sensibly in the middle of the nature-nurture debate, and scientists who care deeply about ending inequality and oppression can at the same time also talk freely about biological differences between the male and female brain and mind. A new theory claims that the female brain is predominantly hard-wired for empathy, and that the male brain is predominantly hard-wired for understanding and building systems. It is known as the empathizing-systemizing (E-S) theory. Empathizing is the drive to identify another person's emotions and thoughts, and to respond to these with an appropriate emotion. The empathizer intuitively figures out how people are feeling, and how to treat people with care

---

7   This paper appeared in "Phi Kappa Phi Forum 2005" (Special issue on the Human Brain); the whole paper is available in appendix 4.

and sensitivity. Systemizing is the drive to analyze and explore a system, to extract underlying rules that govern the behavior of a system; and the drive to construct systems. The "systemizer" intuitively figures out how things work, or what the underlying rules are controlling a system. Systems can be as varied as a pond, a vehicle, a computer, a plant, a library catalogue, a musical instrument, a math equation, or even an army unit. They all operate on inputs and deliver outputs, using rules. According to this new theory, a person (whether male or female) has a particular 'brain type'. There are 3 common brain types: For some individuals, empathizing is stronger than systemizing. This is called a brain of type E, but we can also call it the female brain, because more females than males show this profile. For other individuals, systemizing is stronger than empathizing. This is called a brain of type S, but we can also call it the male brain, because more males than females show this profile. Yet other individuals are equally strong in their systemizing and empathizing. This is called the 'balanced brain', or a brain of type B. The evidence for a female advantage in empathizing comes from many different areas. For example, given a free choice of which toys to play with, more girls than boys will play with dolls, enacting social and emotional themes. When children are put together to play with a little movie player that has only one eye-piece, overall boys tend to get more of their fair share of looking down the eye piece. They just shoulder the other boys out of the way. Or if you leave out those big plastic cars that children can ride on, what you see is that more little boys play the 'ramming' game. They deliberately drive the vehicle into another child. The little girls ride around more carefully, avoiding the other children more often. This suggests the girls are being more sensitive to others. Baby girls, as young as 12 months old, respond more empathically to the distress of other people, showing greater concern through sad looks, sympathetic vocalizations and comforting. This echoes what you find in adulthood: more women report frequently sharing the emotional distress of their friends. Women also show more comforting than men do. When asked to judge when someone might have said something potentially hurtful – a faux pas – girls score higher from at least 7 years old. Women are also more sensitive to facial expressions. They are better at decoding non-verbal communication, picking up subtle nuances from tone of voice or facial expression, or judging a person's character. There is also a sex difference in how aggression is expressed. Males tend to show far more 'direct' aggression (pushing, hitting, punching, etc.,). Females tend to show more 'indirect' (or 'relational', covert) aggression. This includes things like gossip, exclusion, and bitchy remarks. It could be said that to punch someone in the face or to wound them physically requires an even lower level of empathy than a verbal snipe. Two other ways to reveal a person's empathizing skill are to see how they (as a newcomer) join a group of strangers, and to see how they (as a host) react to a new person joining their group. This has been cleverly investigated in children by introducing a new boy or girl to a group who are already playing together. If the newcomer is female, she is more likely to stand and watch for a while, to check out what's going on, and then try to fit in with the ongoing activity. This usually leads to the newcomer being readily accepted into the group. If the newcomer is a boy, he is more likely to hijack the game by trying to change it, directing everyone's attention on to them. And even by the age of 6, girls are better at being a host. They are more attentive to the newcomer. Boys often just ignore the newcomer's attempt to join in. They are more likely to carry on with what they were already doing, perhaps preoccupied by their own interests. How early are such sex differences in empathy evident? Certainly, by 12 months of age, girls make more eye contact than boys. *But a study from Cambridge University shows that at birth, girls look longer at a face, and boys look longer at a suspended mechanical mobile.* Furthermore, the Cambridge team found that how much eye contact children make is in part determined by a biological factor, prenatal testosterone. This has been demonstrated by measuring this hormone in amniotic fluid. Boys, from toddlerhood onwards, are more interested in cars, trucks, planes, guns and swords, building blocks, constructional toys, and mechanical toys - systems. They seem to love putting things together, to build toy towers or towns or vehicles. Boys also enjoy playing with toys that have clear functions – buttons to press, things that will light up, or devices that will cause another object to move. The same sort of pattern is seen in the adult work place. Some occupations are almost entirely male: Metal-working, weapon-making, crafting musical instruments, or the construction industries, such as boat-building. The focus of these occupations is on constructing systems. Professions such as mathematics, physics, and engineering, which require high systemizing, are also largely male-chosen disciplines. Some psychological tests also show the male advantage in systemizing. For example, in the Mental Rotation Test, you're shown two shapes, and asked if one is a rotation or a mirror image of the other. Males are quicker and more accurate on this test. Reading maps has been used as another test of systemizing. Men can learn a route in fewer trials, just from looking at a map, correctly recalling more details about direction and distance. If you ask boys to make a map of an area that they have only visited once, their maps have a more accurate layout of the features in the environment, e.g., showing which landmark is southeast of another. If you ask people to put together a 3-D mechanical apparatus in an assembly task, on average men score higher. Boys are also better at constructing block buildings from 2-D blueprints. These are constructional systems. The male preference for focusing on systems again is evident very early. The Cambridge study found that at one-year old, little boys showed a stronger preference to watch a film of cars (mechanical systems), than a film of a person's face (with lots of emotional expression). Little girls showed the opposite preference. *And at one-day old, little boys look for longer at a mechanical mobile.* Culture and socialization play a role in determining if you develop a male brain (stronger interest in systems) or female brain (stronger interest in empathy). But these studies of infancy strongly suggest that biology also partly determines this. Some of the most convincing evidence for biological causes comes from studies of the effects of hormones. There was a time when women were prescribed a synthetic female hormone (diesthyl-stibestrol), in an attempt to prevent repeated spontaneous miscarriages. Boys born to such women are likely to show more female-typical, empathizing behaviors, such as caring for dolls. And if a female rat is injected at birth with testosterone, she shows faster, more accurate maze learning, compared to a female rat who has not been given such an injection. So masculinizing the rat hormonally improves her spatial systemizing. Some important lessons have been learnt from studies of clinical conditions. Male babies born with IHH (idiopathic hypogonadotrophic hypogonadism) have very small testes (and therefore very low levels of testosterone) and they are worse at spatial aspects of systemizing, relative to normal males. Other male babies born with Androgen Insensitivity (AI) Syndrome (testosterone is an androgen) are also worse at systemizing. Compare these to female babies born with CAH (congenital adrenal hyperplasia), who have unusually high levels of androgens and who have enhanced spatial systemizing. But even leaving aside these clinical conditions, there is evidence for the effects of hormones on the mind in the typical child: A Cambridge study found that toddlers who had lower fetal testosterone had higher levels of eye contact. Eye-contact may be related to sociability and empathizing. And a group of Canadian researchers found that the higher your prenatal testosterone the better you do on the Mental Rotation (systemizing) Test. The E-S theory does not stereotype. Rather, it may help us explain why individuals are typical or atypical for their sex. It may help us understand the childhood neurological conditions of autism and Asperger Syndrome, which appear to be an extreme of the male brain. Such individuals may have impairments in empathizing alongside normal or even talented systemizing. Earlier studies of psychological sex differences have focused on what is sometimes called 'the holy trinity': spatial ability, mathematical ability, and verbal ability. The first two of these are areas where males perform at a higher level, and the last of these typically shows a female advantage. However, spatial and mathematical abilities involve systemizing, and so may simply be further evidence for the E-S theory. Verbal ability may have nothing to do with empathy, in which case this will need to be regarded as an additional dimension along which the sexes differ psychologically. However, good empathizing and good verbal skills both facilitate communication, so that verbal and empathy skills may not be truly independent.

Key references:
S. Baron-Cohen, "The Essential Difference: men, women and the extreme male brain" (Penguin, Allen Lane/ Basic Books, 2003).
D. Kimura, "Sex and Cognition" (MIT Press/Bradford Books, 1997)

Acknowledgements
This article was based on material by the author that first appeared in Gregory, R, (ed) Oxford Companion to the Mind (2nd edition, 2004) Oxford University Press. The author was supported by the MRC UK during the period of this work.

These scientific insights will be used repeatedly in this pamphlet.

I.4 Defense of Motherhood

This pamphlet presents a political program that improves both the economy and the social status of the woman, *beginning by that of the housewife*. The particular importance of the housewife is that she represents the (by far) main factor granting moral education in a society. Modern economies that stubbornly refuse to raise the mother's social status will extinguish with a splendid Darwin's award for suicide stupidity. Since men and women contribute equally to a nation's economy, motherhood should be remunerated[8] to such extent that, women's salaries equal men's.

At this point feminists, a most powerful pressure group that I cannot allow to lose, might respond: "is this not exactly what we have been fighting against, the last half century?" The answer is no, not at all. You have been fighting *for* the social status of women, *not against* the status of housewives. Feminists were too concerned with

---

8   Following a quality criterion, of course

changing society, both men and women, as if they were toys that you can tear down to pieces and later resurrect them. If you do not believe on my authority (which would be not very smart to do anyway), just believe on account of the > 200.000 years of human evolution.

Hence, we have the same final goal, the only difference being that I propose to start from the lower end of the food chain, and you always focused on the higher end. Take for example minimal feminine presence in high-end positions. Of course these decrees "work", in the sense that the proportion of female directives temporarily rises. But this is obviously a short-term effect. The long-term effect destroys what little is left of the social status of women: first, men consider all female directives as fools who got there not because of their talent and potential, but because of a discriminatory gender-law. Think of the mess when minima were to be mandated for LGBT as well. Then every big business would be obliged to have a "deep-state board" and a "window-dressing board".

Second, large enterprises abuse of their female directives as a means to attract young people to apply, while stalling those very female directives in a Kindergarten. Dear feminists, is this what you want?

Of course not. That is why the only *reasonable* option is starting from the bottom of the social status. Why we should begin with paying housewives (rather than top-level ambitious women[9]) is rather obvious, but for those feminists who are not convinced that is the only feasible way, I suggest you read this pamphlet.

---

9   I appreciate women at high directive positions nothing more and mothing less than housewives. Obviously, I would never marry one.

Chapter 1

Genetics and Gender

1.1 Sexual Mosaics

Fig. 1.1: Dutch athletic sprinter Foekje Dillema

Due to a genetic XY-disturbance, my fellow country-
woman and athletic sprinter, Foekje Dillema, was
expelled from the 1950 national team, after she refused a
mandatory sex test in July 1950; she refused the test
because of its extremely humiliating nature. Later
investigations revealed a Y-chromosome in her body cells,
and the analysis showed that she probably was a
46,XX/46,XY mosaic female. She was a humble girl from
a humble village, and never went public again after 1950
because of a deep feeling of shame. "Ze zeggen dat ik geen
meid ben!"[10]

There are at least three categories of people with a
gender-pathology. For sexually healthy LGBT's (i.e.,
pertaining to the sexual standard: female XX or male XY),
some are duped by a significant youth trauma (violation,
beatings), others by false indoctrination. A third category
consists of people pertaining to a sexual minority, like
sexual mosaics and inverted phenotypes. This category
has a sexual pathology. All three categories suffer from a
psychological or psychiatric condition *in causa*, that is, as
a consequence of previous experiences.

---

10   They say I'm not a girl!

1.2 Evolution theory

The big question is: what is true and what false doctrine? I always stick to science, wherever the consensus among the specialists in the field exceeds 90%. Wikipedia, a generally good introduction to scientific subjects, but always subject to the author's own preferences, writes:

> The XY sex-determination system is the sex-determination system found in humans, most other mammals, some insects (Drosophila), some snakes, and some plants (Ginkgo). In this system, the sex of an individual is determined by a pair of sex chromosomes. Females typically have two of the same kind of sex chromosome (XX), and are called the homogametic sex. Males typically have two different kinds of sex chromosomes (XY), and are called the heterogametic sex. [...]
>
> In humans, half of spermatozoons carry X chromosome and the other half Y chromosome. A single gene (SRY) present on the Y chromosome acts as a signal to set the developmental pathway towards maleness. [...] The cells in females, with two X chromosomes, undergo X-inactivation, in which one of the two X chromosomes is inactivated. The inactivated X chromosome remains within a cell as a Barr body.

This is the majority (XX female, XY male) sexual constitution. Exceptions obviously exist:

> Humans, as well as some other organisms, can have a

flawed[11] chromosomal arrangement that is contrary to their phenotypic sex; for example, XX males or XY females (see androgen insensitivity syndrome). Additionally, an abnormal number of sex chromosomes (aneuploidy) may be present, such as Turner's syndrome, Klinefelter's syndrome, [and others]. In most mammals, sex is determined by presence of the Y chromosome. "Female" is the default sex, due to the absence of the Y chromosome. SRY is a sex-determining gene on the Y chromosome in the therians (placental mammals and marsupials). Non-human mammals use several genes on the Y chromosome. Not all male-specific genes are located on the Y chromosome.

From these quotes it is clear that (i) genetically healthy humans are XY-men and XX-women, (ii) genetic exceptions are too many to mention them all within this pamphlet, (iii) the name "phenotypic sex" is a biological misnomer for a "phenotypic gender syndrome", and (iv) the XY-mechanism for sexual differentiation already existed, in a more primitive way, in fish. The last point implies that human sexual differentiation is not something that occurred some *millions* of years ago in evolution, but *billions* of years ago. For non-scientists, this difference is quite hard to grasp. To take a trivial example, dinosaurs lived millions of years ago. Billions of

---

11   Adjective added by myself, that is, absent in the Wikipedia quote

years ago about all the world population consisted of microbes.

Clearly, the XY-sex differentiation mechanism precedes Homo Sapiens by billions of years. It obviously entails a huge number of biological and behavioral characteristics differentiating females from males. That is not something a bunch of unhappy women can change by talking, protesting, or manifesting. *Who does not accept this, cannot but accept that (s)he thinks to know it better than a 90% majority in the specific scientific field.*

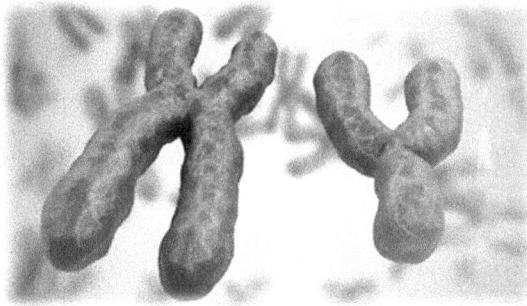

Figure: 1.2: An artist's impression of the X and Y chromosomes, respectively.

Do you notice any difference? By the way, the nucleic acids inside the chromosomes are completely different, too. The artist was not able to image that difference, alas.

1.3 Suicide

The word "gender" is a syndrome-related medical term, just like "homosexual", "lesbian", "bisexual", or "transsexual" (LGBT). For sure, in the very large majority of cases, the terms have nothing whatever in common with the LGBT's chromosomal constitution. Medical science is quite clear on the subject: LGBT's have a right to psychiatric care.

This Section is full of equations. The reader may skip it, upon reading only the main conclusion, namely, that the growth rate in annual suicides has two main components: the LGBT community itself accounted for a suicide increase in 2016 of 5547 individuals, and children of LGBT mothers for 793 individuals. The total suicide number per year was 440 thousand in 2016, and the total suicide rate was 7 thousand per year; that is, in 2017 it would rise to 447 thousand, in 2018 to 554 thousand. See you back Chapter 2!

Psychiatric conditions are usually related to higher suicide rates. Let us have a closer look at the numbers. Among youth who identify as sexual minorities, the suicide rate has been estimated to be two to seven times greater than among heterosexual youth, as deduced by

Ann Haas and colleagues.[12] Haas suggests that such a range exists because records of death rarely include a person's sexual orientation. That is only part of the truth of course. The other part is that the LGBT community actively hides suicide statistics, in order to obstruct and even penalize the scientific claim of a pathology.

The National Survey of Family Growth is a nationally representative, multi-year survey of teenagers and adults aged 15–44. The sexual orientation items are presented only to interviewees over age 18. The results shown in Table 1.3, separately for women and men, suggest that the percentage of American adults identifying as heterosexual was 94% throughout the years from 2006 to 2013. Since this is a quite long period, we may safely assume that this number has not changed significantly over the last years.

According to Gallup, the percentage of American adults identifying as LGBT was 3.5% in 2012, 4.1% in 2016, 4.5% in 2017. This is compatible with the National Survey, as the total of non-heterosexuals of 6% also includes people who have both hetero and non-hetero sexual relations.

---

12 Ann Haas & 25 colleagues, "Suicide and Suicide Risk in Lesbian, Gay, Bisexual, and Transgender Populations: Review and Recommendations", Journal of Homosexuality 58 (2011) pages 10–51

WOMEN	Lesbian	Bisexual	Trans	Hetero	Unknown
2002	1.3%	2.8%	3.8%	90.3%	1.8%
2006-2010	1.2%	3.9%	0.4%	93.6%	0.8%
2011-2013	1.3%	5.5%	—	92.3%	0.9%
MEN	Gay	Bisexual	Trans	Hetero	Unknown
2002	2.3%	1.8%	3.9%	90.2%	1.8%
2006-2010	1.8%	1.2%	0.2%	95.6%	1.2%
2011-2013	1.9%	2.0%	—	95.1%	1.0%

Table 1.3: National Survey of Family Growth figures on sexual orientation

On the other hand, Fig. 1.4 shows the total (that is, summed over all sexual orientations) suicide fractions (misnamed "rates") in the US over the last ten years. The fractions grow with a mainly linear rate of 2 suicides per million people per year. In this section I will try to connect that data provided by Ann Haas, Gallup, and the suicide fractions registered in all States of the US. The total suicide number $N_{[s]}(\Delta y)$ for sexual orientation "s" in year "$2000 + \Delta y$" is a product of a fraction $f_{[s]}(\Delta y)$ for sexual orientation "s" in year "$2000 + \Delta y$" and the total US population, $P_{[US]}(\Delta y)$:

(1) $N_{[s]}(\Delta y) = f_{[s]}(\Delta y)P_{[US]}(\Delta y)$

Deriving this equation to the differential year (Δy) yields, according to the chain rule:

(2) $\dot{N}_{[s]}(\Delta y) = f_{[s]}(\Delta y)\dot{P}_{[US]}(\Delta y) + \dot{f}_{[s]}(\Delta y)\dot{P}_{[US]}(\Delta y)$

The dot on top of a physical quantity indicates its derivative to time in units of years (yr). Hence, the dot turns a physical quantity into a rate of that quantity.

The sum of suicide fractions is shown in Fig. 1.4.

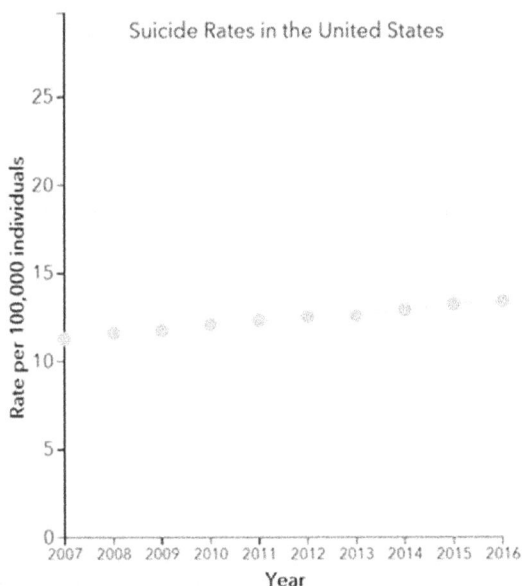

Figure 1.4: Total suicide fractions (misnamed "rates") in the US during ten consecutive years. *The term "rate" (in both the title and the y-axis legend) is inappropriate, as it exclusively refers to temporal*

---

derivatives. Consequently, the "rate of suicide fractions" is given by the slope of the line.

Figure 1.4 shows that, between 2007 and 2016, the suicide fractions vary approximately linearly with time:

(3) $f_{[US]}(\Delta y) = f_{[US]}(0yr) + \Delta y \dot{f}_{[US]}$

with the fraction growth rate independent of time and equal to $\dot{f}_{[US]} = 2 * 10^{-6}/yr$, whereas the total fraction at reference year 2000 equal to $f_{[US]}(0yr) = 10^{-4}$. The total US population in that same year was approximately $P_{[US]}(0) = 280 * 10^6$, and its yearly growth rate $\dot{P}_{[US]} = 2.3 * 10^6/yr$. Substituting the above numbers into the chain-rule equation, one obtains:

(4) $\dot{N}_{[US]}(\Delta y) = \dfrac{790}{yr} + 13.2\dfrac{\Delta y}{yr^2}$

The nineteenth century did not yet know the LGBT phenomenon, although homosexuality always existed. Since it had little influence on society, the homosexual suicide fractions can safely be put to zero, without distorting reality too much. Hence, we attribute all suicides to the heterosexual category:

(5) $f_{[hetero]}(-100) = 5 * 10^{-5}$

In the simplest possible model, the suicide fraction was constant throughout the 19th century, which instantly changed into a linearly increasing fraction. Such a simplistic model is a lowest order approximation of reality, in which the transition from a vanishing fraction rate to the present one of $\dot{f}_{[US]} = 2 * 10^{-6}/yr$ obviously occurred smoothly. Since we are not interested in details, but in a rough estimation, we make the simplistic model consistent by calculating the year in which the constant fraction suddenly changed into a linearly increasing fraction. That flop-year

$(2000 + \Delta y_{[flop]})$ obeys the equation

$$(6) \; 5 * 10^{-5} = 10^{-4} + 2 * 10^{-6} \frac{\Delta y_{[flop]}}{yr}$$

whence

$$(7) \; \Delta y_{[flop]} = -\frac{5*10^{-5}}{2*10^{-6}} yr = -25 \; yr$$

meaning that the derived discontinuity occurs in the year 1975, roughly 10 years after the sexual revolution. This is right within our ballpark, and confirms the utility of the simplistic model. The conclusion from this simplistic model is that all non-hetero sexual orientations together (LGBT) account for the fractional annual growth rate of $2 * 10^{-6}/yr$. Hence, by the year 2025 the annual LGBT suicide fraction is approximately 10^{-4}, which is twice that of heterosexuals.

Since the population fraction of LGBT & other non-purely-heterosexual people is about 10%, *our simplistic model implies that in 2025 the suicide probability in the LGBT community is about 20 times higher than in the purely-heterosexual community.*

Ann Haas found a proportionality factor "between 2 and 7". Given my estimate of 20, one can easily infer to how much pressure she was subjected by political correctness. This high pressure obviously corresponds to long-sustained high levels of brainwashing. High levels of brainwashing require enormous funds. Who is able and willing to provide these funds? EZ is clearly trying to hide, with whatever means, the horrible LGBT truth. LGBT is not a free choice, but a horrible disorder, which reduces mankind to despair and morbidity. The only way back is that of the Catholic church: loving the LGBT community, without however withholding them the plain truth: LGBT is not just another brain disorder, like OCD and so many others. It is a brain disorder that makes you decide to end your life before you reach your menopause/midlife crisis, or whatever this is called by the LGBT community.

Among genetically healthy adults, a heterosexual orientation is the healthiest one. This is what the above numbers tell us, or rather, shout out. That is what all primitive societies shout out. The Catholic-invaded

Southern America is full of ancient races and mixtures of all possible percentages. Plenty of gender evidence there. Not so in Northern America and Canada, where Deism wiped *all native races* off the map in a mere century. That is why looking back to the Catholic feminism of Te Ata is not all that stupid.[13]

---

13 Too bad, the suicide numbers of the American tribes, before the arrival of European Deism, are not known. In contrast to what Hollywood movies want you to believe, the large-scale scalp chasers were Deist intruders, not native Americans. Official rewards on native scalps reduced the natives to an outlawed animal species. Deism did exactly the same in South-Africa (my own country coined the term "apartheid"), and our South-African extremist Calvinist ministers duly preached God's rejection of negro's, on the basis of an obscure old-testament quote involving the death of Abel due to his evil brother, Cain, who turned black after his sin. This immediately unveils the much hailed Dutch "tolerance" as a sad historic lie. I hope, for the extremist Calvinists in question, that Abel had procreated before dying under Cain's blows. Else, they are descendants of Cain, too, according to their own idiotic theology. Or should I say, animal theology?

1.4 Transgenderism

The next paper, written by Meredith Wadman, discusses a fratricide war in the discipline of gender identity. It is the same kind of war that occurred in the discipline of climate change, so vehemently fought by the overtly non-academic Al Gore.[14] By now his role is completely finished, as climate change has definitively been attributed to non-human factors, by all professional scientists in the field (except, of course, the EZ-created, Idiotic Panel for Climate Change).

'Rapid onset' of transgender identity ignites storm

Summary: Critics charge a psychological study is biased, but others say politics is inhibiting science
by Meredith Wadman[15]

A study describing "rapid onset gender dysphoria" (ROGD) in teens and young adults—a sudden unease

---

14 No shame for him. As everybody knows, the Florida elections were fraudulent. EZ needed an overall loser as a President, because any real man would not have allowed 9/11 to happen so smoothly. So EZ proposed the climate scam to the much more talented Al Gore.

15 http://science.sciencemag.org/ on September 11, 2018

with the gender they were assigned at birth—has infuriated transgender activists while sparking a debate about academic freedom. Critics of the paper, published last month in *PLOS ONE* by physician-scientist Lisa Littman of Brown University, call it a flawed study that reflects an anti-transgender agenda, in part because it suggests some cases may be the result of "social contagion." Brown and the journal have both distanced themselves from the paper, drawing charges that they surrendered to political pressure. The study remains freely available, but last week, *PLOS ONE* announced it is conducting a post-publication investigation of its methodology and analysis. "This is not about suppressing academic freedom or scientific research. This is about the scientific content itself—whether there is anything that needs to be looked into or corrected," *PLOS ONE* Editor-in-Chief Joerg Heber in San Francisco, California, told *Science* in an interview. Also last week, Brown officials removed the university's press release highlighting the paper from its website. Bess Marcus, dean of Brown's School of Public Health, wrote in an open letter that the university acted "in light of questions raised about research design and data collection related to the study." She added that people in the Brown community have raised concerns that the study's conclusions "could be used to discredit efforts to support transgender youth and invalidate the perspectives of members of the transgender community." Brown's move prompted Jeffrey Flier, a former dean of Harvard Medical School in Boston and a professor of medicine there, to say in a tweet: "This is a sad day for @Brown University, and an indictment of the integrity of their academic and administrative leadership." In an interview, Flier called elements of Marcus's statement "anti-intellectual" and "completely antithetical to academic freedom," and said he found it "horrifying" that Brown failed to defend Littman. A petition urging Brown and PLOS ONE "to resist ideologically based attempts to squelch controversial research evidence" had garnered nearly 3900 signatures by early this week. The controversy comes after several years of rapid growth in the number of adolescents being referred to clinics specializing in gender dysphoria in North America and Europe. For instance, a paper published in April in the Archives of Sexual Behavior analyzed 2009–16 data from a U.K. specialist service that is the largest in the world. The study described recent, dramatic growth in both total adolescent referrals and the proportion of those patients who were designated female at birth (see graph, right). In the past, the majority of patients at such clinics had been designated male at birth. The authors wrote that their findings "reflect a general trend of inversion in sex ratios" in adolescents seeking treatment in several developed countries. They speculated that causes might include that "coming out … may be easier for birth-assigned females than it is for birth-assigned males" as awareness of transgender identity grows. But, "It is not possible to say with any confidence why" the sex inversion is happening, says Polly Carmichael, the paper's senior author and director of the Gender Identity Development Service at The Tavistock and Portman NHS Foundation Trust in London. Michael Bailey, an academic psychologist who studies sexual orientation and gender dysphoria at Northwestern

University in Evanston, Illinois, says his colleagues who treat gender dysphoria "all tell me that their primary group these days are adolescent females who were not known to be gender dysphoric [in childhood].

This kind of case virtually never happened until recently—even a decade ago you didn't see them. I don't know what else to call this but an epidemic." In 2016, spurred by accounts of sudden transitions among young people, Littman surveyed parents she recruited from three websites where she had read such descriptions by parents: 4thWaveNow, Transgender Trend, and YouthTransCritical Professionals. The first two are gathering places for parents concerned by their children's exploration of a transgender identity. (The third website is closed to nonmembers.) According to 256 parents who responded to the 90-question survey, none of their children —83% of whom were designated female at birth— had symptoms that matched the professionally defined diagnosis of gender dysphoria during childhood. The finding suggests "that not all [young people] presenting at these vulnerable ages are correct in their self-assessment of the cause of their symptoms," Littman wrote. She suggested some young people may be seeking gender transition to escape other emotional difficulties. But transgender activists furiously dispute the existence of ROGD, and Littman's description of it, which is the first in the literature. They argue that what may seem a "rapid onset" to parents is likely the result of a lengthy internal process in children. "What's 'rapid' about ROGD is parents' sudden awareness and assessment of their child's gender dysphoria," the Oakland, California-based transgender writer and

former developmental biologist Julia Serano wrote in
a critical essay last month. She argues that Littman's
paper provides no evidence for the existence of
ROGD. She added in an interview that others have
already embraced ROGD for ideological reasons — "to
do an end run around existing trans health practices
that advocate for supporting and affirming trans
kids." The most explosive of Littman's findings may be
that among the young people reported on, more than
one-third had friendship groups in which 50% or more
of the youths began to identify as transgender in a
similar time frame. This, Littman writes, was more
than 70 times the expected prevalence of
transgender identity in young adults. She
hypothesizes that "social contagion" may be a key
driver of some cases of the purportedly rapid onset
dysphoria. To trans activists and some clinicians, such
a suggestion denies the inner experience of
transgender youths and risks stigmatizing and
further isolating them from their peers and
supportive resources. Critics also assailed Littman for
failing to recruit participants from other websites
supportive of transgender youth and for not
interviewing such youths themselves. Littman
defended her choice of sites, writing in an email to
Science that in order to find cases of ROGD, she
targeted the only three sites where she had seen
parents discussing something like it. "I would have
rejected this manuscript outright for its
methodological flaws and also its bias," says Diane
Ehrensaft, director of mental health at the Child and
Adolescent Gender Center Clinic at the University of
California, San Francisco's Benioff Children's
Hospital; she treats transgender young people as a

clinical psychologist and has reviewed scientific papers for journals. The paper's implication that gender exploration "is simply a fad whipped up by peer influence" should not be taken as authentic, she argues. "It negates the experience of many transgender youth." But Ray Blanchard, a professor of psychiatry at the University of Toronto in Canada who worked for 15 years in a gender identity clinic that screened candidates for sex reassignment surgery, says the paper points to a clear phenomenon. "Many clinicians in North America and elsewhere have been seeing such patients," Blanchard, who worked with adults, wrote in an email, "and it has been speculated that this subgroup is one reason for the predominance of adolescent females now being seen in North America and elsewhere." Blanchard added, "No one can deny the clinical reality" of a new subgroup of adolescents, mainly female, who experience gender dysphoria after showing no behavioral signs of it during childhood. In the study, Littman acknowledged its limitations. "Like all first descriptive studies, additional studies will be needed to replicate the findings," she wrote. She told *Science* that in upcoming research she plans to recruit parent-teen pairs in cases where the teenager experienced ROGD that later resolved.

CHAPTER 2
Evolution and Male Dominance

Why would a woman want to be like a man, given that men's suicide rates more than triple that of women? That would imply choosing for decreased odds of happiness. In this chapter I present the three most ridiculous kinds of feminism. I believe they are EZ-steered. Moreover, I do not judge the women presented in this chapter (and showing themselves this way on social media), who have my sincerest sympathy. I only judge the underlying ideologies.

2.1 Soft Body-Feminism: Trying to Look Like Men by Growing Muscles

Figure 2.1: Donna Gittings, a quite muscled woman.

She does not look too happy, though.

2.2 Hard Body-Feminism: Trying to be an Asexual Bunch of Muscles

Figure 2.2: Iranian Shirin, a beautifully smiling girl before (above panel), and a thoroughly bored asexual primate, after her hormone cure (lower panel).

Donna Gittings only betrays a personal issue. It is quite possible that she does not aspire at all at being like a man. Nobody knows. Possibly, she does not know herself. The psychology of healthy people is already incomprehensible, let alone of people with an evident psychological condition. On the other hand, having a psychological condition is common to everybody,[16] so nothing pathological in the case of Donna, methinks.

The Iranian Shirin, takes so many hormones that her femininity disappears completely, and she ends up looking like an asexual primate. This *is* pathological.

2.3 Aggressive Feminism: Taking Pleasure in Humiliating Mothers

A very well-known Dutch example of a feminist whose main theme was to humiliate traditional housewives is Heleen Mees. The poor woman never realized that she lacks the very basics of femininity. From her writings I have never been able to deduce any sign of intelligence, possibly due to her mono-thematic scolding. Life was kind

---

16   Psychologists themselves are a significant risk group

to her when she was young and beautiful.[17] But once in her forties, further botoxing did more harm than good, and she desperately tried to fix a once-married Dutch banker, Willem Buiter. The poor banker paid his multiple infidelities to his earlier wives at a huge price. He barely won a process against Heleen for obsessive personal harassment and threats against his wife and children from his first wife (what a mess you made of your life, Willem, for the mere reason of primarily running after your dick). In mafia-less circumstances, Heleen would have been placed immediately in a psychiatric institution, end of story. Now that EZ got interested in the case, Heleen is successfully suing the banker for ruining her "reputation".[18] By the way, contemporary Dutch

17 Blinding beauty has nothing whatsoever in common with femininity

18 All judges suddenly seem to agree that the banker went far beyond the law. They obviously do not agree, but give me the name of a single judge in the US who has not been threatened by EZ. Or of a president. You know what happened to those presidents that did not convert into EZ's pawns: Ronald Reagan, John F. Kennedy, and all presidents who were killed in the history of the US. They were all presidents who tried to shut down EZ's Federal Reserve. As you certainly know, John F. got the bullet a few weeks after he started printing, on the government's authority, his first US national dollars. EZ had no choice but to kill him, since the government's dollars were backed by the government's gold and silver reserves, while the Fed's dollars were backed by a big air balloon.

feminism, like Stalinism, deleted all records of Heleen Mees. If you would ask them, Heleen never existed.

Yet she existed, and still continues to do so. In the year 2013, journalist Jon Swaine wrote in *the Telegraph*:

Citigroup Buiter's ex-mistress sent threatening emails and lewd photos

Willem Buiter, one of Britain's most respected economists, was bombarded with threatening emails and lewd photographs by his former mistress after their affair ended, it has been alleged. Mr. Buiter, the London-based chief economist of Citigroup, was stalked by Heleen Mees for years after she recruited him to help her with a PhD dissertation, according to court documents in the US. Ms. Mees, a Dutch lawyer and economist, is accused of sending married Mr. Buiter pictures of her pleasuring herself and asking him in an email: "What can I do to make it right? Shall I lick your balls? As their alleged relationship soured, the 44-year-old is also said to have sent Mr. Buiter, 63, a photograph of dead birds and to have said in another email: "Hope your plane falls out of the sky". Ms. Mees was arrested on Monday and charged at Manhattan criminal court with five counts of stalking and harassment. She is being held on $5,000 (£3,280) bail, and is due to appear in court on Friday. She faces a up to a year in prison if convicted. Mr. Buiter, a former member of the Bank of England's monetary policy committee who holds British citizenship and was educated at Cambridge, is a columnist for The Financial Times.

It is alleged that he first met Ms. Mees in London in 2008, when he was working as a professor at the London School of Economics and she was working on a doctorate in economic policy. She later paid tribute in her thesis to "Willem Buiter, who was so kind to meet with me", and even dedicated the publication to the Dutch-born economist, declaring it to be: "For Willem". Vaneshka Hyacinthe, Ms. Mees's court-appointed lawyer, claimed in court that the pair then "had a long-standing relationship", and records show that emails in fact went "in both directions".

However, New York prosecutors allege that Ms. Mees, a multilingual feminist activist, has sent Mr. Buiter more than 1,000 emails since July 2011, once asking him: "Shall we adopt a child?" Ms. Mees "would also send him naked pictures of other women", according to a complaint filed to the court by prosecutors. She is accused of also targeting Mr. Buiter's wife, Anne Sibert, a professor of economics at the University of London and a former senior official at the Bank of Iceland. Mr. Buiter's children from his first marriage – David, 22, and Elizabeth, 19 – were also subjected to emails from Ms. Mees, according to prosecutors. "The defendant's actions have caused him severe annoyance and alarm, and to fear for his physical safety and for the safety of his wife and children," they said. While Mr. Buiter is based in London, he has a $4.3 million (£2.8 million) flat on Manhattan's Upper West Side, and received the emails at his New York home, it is alleged. He told Ms. Mees "to stop contacting him and sent a cease and desist letter" in February, prosecutors said. Yet she "has continued to contact him, and he has received several hundred emails from the defendant since" then. Judge Robert Mandelbaum issued Ms. Mees, who lives in a flat in an affluent neighborhood of Brooklyn, with an order of protection that bans her from contacting Mr. Buiter and his family. "Do not call them, do not go to their home, school, businesses, place of employment," the judge told her. "No email, no text messages, instant messages, no phone calls, letters, fax or voice messages". Mr. Buiter passed a request for comment to a spokesman for Citigroup, who said: "I'm going to decline to comment on an employee's personal matters".

The Bloomberg/EPA photograph showing Mees and Buiter has been taken off the Telegraph website.

In March 2014, the court decided that the case against Mees was to be dismissed in one year provided that she complies with two conditions. Later that year, in September 2014, Mees responded by filing for damages against Buiter. From then on, Buiter was a mere judges' playing ball.

Dutch economist Heleen Mees (accused of cyber-stalking Willem Buiter) in a nail salon a few days after her release from jail.

Brooklyn plumber Leon Alfonso, the man who paid $5,000 to bail out ex-NYU professor Mees from jail, said he had not heard from Mees, but did not expect her to contact him. (Photo: Joe Marino/NY Daily News via Getty Images)

A Brooklyn plumber, who never even knew Mees, bails her out, while expecting no sign of gratitude. This is as mafia as it can be! *But which mafia would be interested in keeping alive a stupid ideological myth, which is a shame for all women?* Given the demonic immorality of Mees' moves, I fear only EZ is a credible candidate.

2.4 Altruistic Feminism

Te Ata's feminism differs from all other kinds in that it is not primarily egotistical. It is concerned with the welfare of all women, irrespective of faith, race, and political opinions. This is the only feminism I take seriously. All other forms do not even merit a nice name like "feminism": they should be called versions of female solipsism. Once we agree on the primary goal of feminism, to wit, increasing the happiness of women, one can have a meaningful discussion. As already mentioned, pushing women to be(have) like men (whose suicides ratios are 3.5 times the females'), is the worst suggestion one can come up with. There must exist positive reasons, taken from femininity, that feminism should try to achieve, such that both the average happiness of women and their respect in society are increased.

Sorry to say so, *but women should do an effort in believing they can achieve what society considers an illusion.* This pamphlet will try to convince women that, *yes, they can* make a difference in the social appreciation. This is the subject of Chapter 3.

Sorry to say so again, but most women have not the faintest idea about what Original Sin did to men. ABBA sings it out loud in "take a chance on me", though it's not the AA girls, but the BB boys who wrote the text "afraid of a love affair".[19] To say it quite bluntly, men want free sex without "love affairs", that is, without any lasting love bonds.

Only femininity seems to understand that men *think* they only need sex to be happy. Femininity understands that this is nothing different from kids who *think* they will be happy with a constant influx of sweets, or from women who *think* they will be happy when they have 150 pairs of shoes. *Feminism does not want to understand any of these ideas.* Feminism is, seen through men's eyes, about the lowest level women can reach: crying out loud because men do not take them seriously. What is more self-degrading? Taking a public brown shower? Obviously, men *crave* for feminists, because they are not mentally ripe, and after hearing out all their silly complaints, those very feminists will do anything to sexually please that man. So let us leave the traditional feminists' frustrations and get back to reality.

---

19   The song is about a girl who feels left single: "If you're all alone when the pretty birds have flown — Honey I'm still free — Take a chance on me — Gonna do my very best and it ain't no lie — If you put me to the test, if you let me try." Next the girl reveals how deep she has fallen: "You want me to leave it there, afraid of a love affair — But I think you know — That I can't let go.

CHAPTER 3
Machiavellian Policy

The only factor granting social respect on our planet is money, no matter what feminists think about it. Femininity knows that after her 35th, most of the sexual attraction is gone. Those girls who do not have a solid husband by then, only complicate their lives and are easy prey to BB-boys and depressions. Machiavelli will teach us the solution to this mainly biological problem.

3.1 About My Pen Name

As most of the readership probably knows, Niccolò Machiavelli is the Renaissance writer of "Il Principe" ("The Prince"), a quite immoral handbook of power acquisition. Wikipedia offers the following introductory text:[20]

Niccolò di Bernardo dei Machiavelli (3 May 1469 – 21 June 1527) was an Italian diplomat, politician, historian, philosopher, humanist, writer, playwright and poet of the Renaissance period. He has often been called the father of modern political science. For many years he was a senior official in the Florentine Republic, with responsibilities in diplomatic and military affairs. He also wrote comedies, carnival songs, and poetry. His personal correspondence is renowned by Italian scholars. He was secretary to the Second Chancery of the Republic of Florence from 1498 to 1512, when the Medici were out of power. He wrote his most well-known work The Prince (Il Principe) in 1513, having been exiled from city affairs. Machiavellianism is widely used as a negative term to characterize unscrupulous politicians of the sort Machiavelli described most famously in The Prince. Machiavelli described immoral behavior, such as dishonesty and the killing of innocents, as being normal and effective in politics. He even seemed to encourage it in some situations. The book gained notoriety due to claims that it teaches "evil recommendations to tyrants to help them maintain their power". The term Machiavellian is often associated with political deceit, deviousness, and realpolitik. On the other hand, many commentators,

---

20 https://en.wikipedia.org/wiki/Niccol%C3%B2_Machiavelli

such as Baruch Spinoza, Jean-Jacques Rousseau and Denis Diderot, have argued that Machiavelli was actually a republican, even when writing The Prince, and his writings were an inspiration to Enlightenment proponents of modern democratic political philosophy. In one place, for example, he noted his admiration for the selfless Roman dictator Cincinnatus.

Everybody has his or her own moral code, and mine does not approve of certain aspects of Machiavelli's Prince. However, this pamphlet is about the very same subject, though specialized to the fight of women for an equal social status. *Whenever I suggest to act in Machiavelli's spirit, I only refer to smart but morally correct means of achieving one's goals, be they legal or illegal.*

The present chapter is quite difficult to understand, for most people in general, and for women in particular. Since mammal females have been under male dominance for hundreds of millions of years, their brains are not hard-wired for power issues.[21] Lionesses do the chasing, and lions do the eating. This is so today, and it was so at the birth of the lion species. Lionesses wait for lunch until the male had its fill. Lion's brains are hardwired for

---

21 With Bonobo's, bees, and many other species this stereotype is not applicable

eliminating competing males, and lionesses' brains are hard-wired for the survival and education of their offspring. If you happen to find yourself alone on a Safari, car gone, tent stolen, and ask yourself how to get to the civilized world with a reasonable state of bodily health, you'd better encounter a lion than a lioness. High odds that the lion has its fill, and leaves you alone. Encounter a lioness, and you are as sure as dead. The same holds for primates, too, of which humans are but a tiny branch.[22]

For the very first time in sexed animal archeology, in humans, the physically weaker sex is able to compete with the stronger. This is historically unique,[23] including the bonobo's. It has never happened before on planet earth, in not a single known sexed animal species.

Too bad, half a century of feminism produced nothing that helped increase the social status of women: on TV, young females are often shown for nothing but their bodily attributes. Young feminists are being pissed off by Milo in such a humiliating way, that one cannot but think of fraud. Meanwhile, women and children trafficking has

---

22 The only exceptions are pets, and they are in no way similar to wild-life animals.

23 In chimpanzees, our closest primate species, such a development is completely unthinkable (except for Jane Goodall, of course, as she insists on being the stupidest of all researchers of animal behavior).

increased like an exploding volcano. The main problem here is that feminists seem unable to distinguish between the ideal and the way to get there. One thing is a goal, another thing are the means for achieving a goal. Before getting into Machiavelli's classroom, we will first have a closer look at the relevant facts (relevant for improving the social status of women).

3.2 Economic Facts

The USA and many other "first-world" countries share the following five facts.

- Women contribute equally to economic growth as men.[24] Muscular strength only makes a difference in prison, and in the worst paid jobs.

- The US suicides are increasing with 2 million people per year Hence, the *proportion of suicide growth* is way higher than the *proportion of population growth*. In my simplistic view this is due mainly to an increasing lack of motherly love.

---

24 At least during the last three centuries

- Women are underrepresented with respect to men in leading functions.

- Motherly care is only valued on the personal level, not on the social level.

A linear fit shows that the population increased about 2.3 million people per year in the past 70 years. A bit less than half the number is due to immigration (0.9 million per year). The nations intrinsic growth is therefore 1.4 million per year. *Given the US birth rate of 1.9, the contribution of newborns would show an intrinsic decrease of population of 5% per generation (say 30 years), which is about 0.5 million per year.* This means that a growth of more than 1.45 million is due to increasing aging of the US population pyramid.

Below is a graph representing the total US population during the last seven decennia.[25] Indeed, the prognoses until 2050 do not lie: by 2050, the median age will have increased by 4 years, the fertility rate will have stabilized to 1.91, and the net increase of population is down to 0.5 million.

---

25 http://www.worldometers.info/world-population/us-population/

United States Population (1950 - 2018)

——— U.S.A. Population

300,000,000

200,000,000

100,000,000

1970   1980   1990   2000   2010

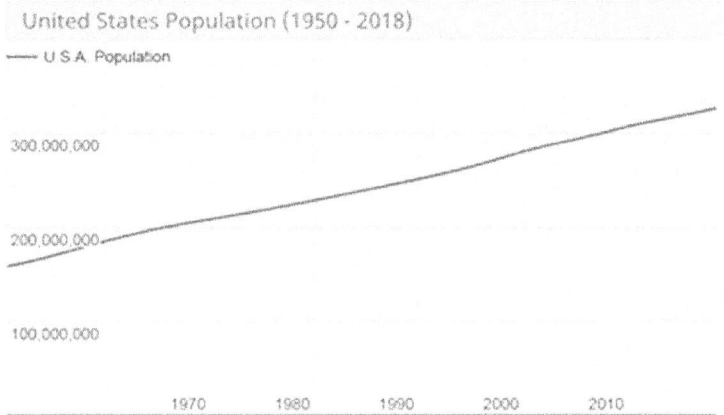

Figure 3.1: Total US population during the last 70 years.

Consequently, the ageing effect will lead to a decrease of the intrinsic growth rate from 1.4 million in 2020 to 0.5 million in 2050. Another 30 years, and America's population will be in free fall if no urgent strategic decisions are made. America will be a piece of cake for China.

United States Population Forecast

Year	Population	Yearly % Change	Yearly Change	Migrants (net)	Median Age	Fertility Rate	Density (P/Km²)	Urban Pop %	Urban Population
2020	331,431,534	0.71 %	2,300,474	900,000	38.3	1.89	36	84.1 %	278,758,373
2025	343,255,846	0.70 %	2,364,862	950,001	39.0	1.89	38	85.1 %	292,221,946
2030	354,711,670	0.66 %	2,291,165	1,000,000	39.8	1.90	39	86.1 %	305,356,412
2035	365,033,872	0.58 %	2,064,440	1,000,000	40.6	1.90	40	87.0 %	317,656,011
2040	374,068,752	0.49 %	1,806,976	1,000,000	41.2	1.91	41	88.0 %	329,038,034
2045	382,058,853	0.42 %	1,598,020	1,000,000	41.7	1.91	42	88.9 %	339,780,873
2050	389,591,663	0.39 %	1,506,562	1,000,000	42.0	1.91	43	89.9 %	350,338,147

Figure 3.2: Prognoses for the US population until 2050

The non-urban population density presently is 18%, which implies a non-urban population density of less than 8 people per square kilometer. This reduces the US to a huge natural park with a few densely populated cities. Was there really no place for native Americans?

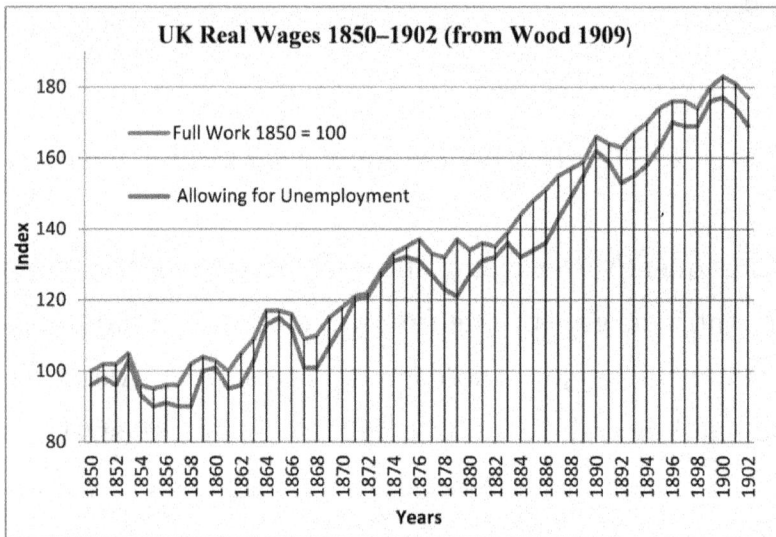

UK Real Wages 1850–1902 (from Wood 1909)

Figure 3.3: Real Wages in the UK in the 20th century

As one can see, they rose from 100 points in 1850 to 180 in 1900. This implies an average relative growth of 1.2% per year.

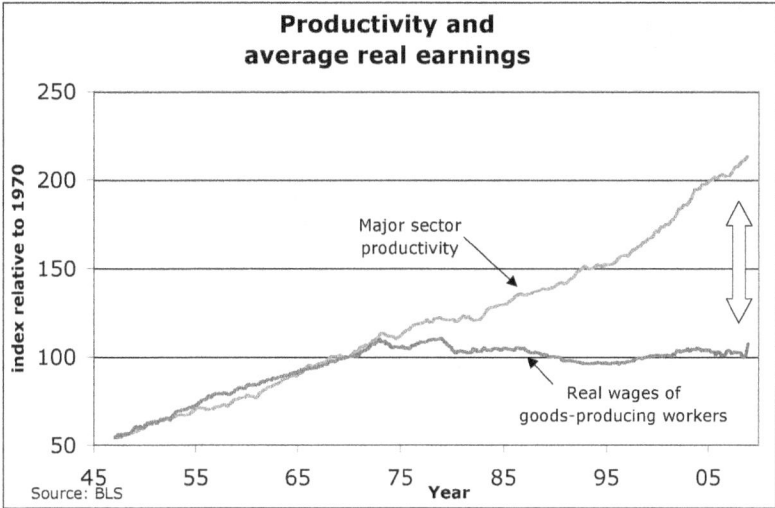

Figure 3.4: US Productivity and average real earnings.[26]

During the years 1945-1973 the productivity and real earnings rose together at a similar pace in the US, too. The sector productivity kept on rising, from 1973 through 2008 with a relative growth rate of 2.4% per year, double the growth of the UK in the temporal bracket from 1850 to 1900. However, it is only too bad that the figure does not mention that on 15 August 1971, the United States unilaterally terminated convertibility of the US dollar to gold, effectively bringing the Bretton Woods system[27] to

---

26 https://en.wikipedia.org/wiki/Personal_income_in_the_
United_States

27 Preparing to rebuild the international economic system while
World War II was still raging, 730 delegates from all 44 allied nations

an end and rendering the dollar a so-called "fiat" (uncovered) currency. This action, referred to as the Nixon shock, created the situation in which the U.S. dollar became a reserve currency used by many states. At the same time, many fixed currencies (such as the pound sterling) also became free-floating.

Clearly, the 65+ bracket has the largest political power. The gap between 65- and 65+ is disproportional.

———————————————

gathered at the Mount Washington Hotel in Bretton Woods, New Hampshire, United States, for the United Nations Monetary and Financial Conference, also known as the Bretton Woods Conference. The delegates deliberated during 1–22 July 1944, and signed the Bretton Woods agreement on its final day. Setting up a system of rules, institutions, and procedures to regulate the international monetary system, these accords established the International Monetary Fund (IMF) and the International Bank for Reconstruction and Development (IBRD), which today is part of the World Bank Group. The United States, which controlled two thirds of the world's gold, insisted that the Bretton Woods system rest on both gold and the US dollar. Soviet representatives attended the conference but later declined to ratify the final agreements, charging that the institutions they had created were "branches of Wall Street" (read: the US banking mafia headed by Rothschild). These organizations became operational in 1945 after a sufficient number of countries had ratified the agreement.

Summarizing, the US have four huge economic challenges to face:

First, the EZ drama of abandoning the Bretton-Woods agreement in 1971 literally stalled workers' wages. From then on EZ, the US parasite, was creaming off increasingly part of American workers' wages, amounting to 50% in 2008. By blunt extrapolation, this cream-off percentage disappearing in the American EZ-parasite's pockets is about 60% of the US GDP. Integrating over the past, EZ is, financially, at least 3 times the size of the US. Since President Woodrow Wilson, EZ is US' deep state, sucking American households' like a bloodthirsty vampire.

Second, the US are presently nearing the most age-deformed age pyramid. Consequently, 65+ aged people largely determine taxing. They suffocate all 65-, with youngsters the most heavily duped. Moreover, growing medical care and investigation (mostly directed to the 65+ bracket) distorts the demographic tables, hiding the fact that, within a century, the American intrinsic (i.e. subtracting immigration) population will start falling dramatically.

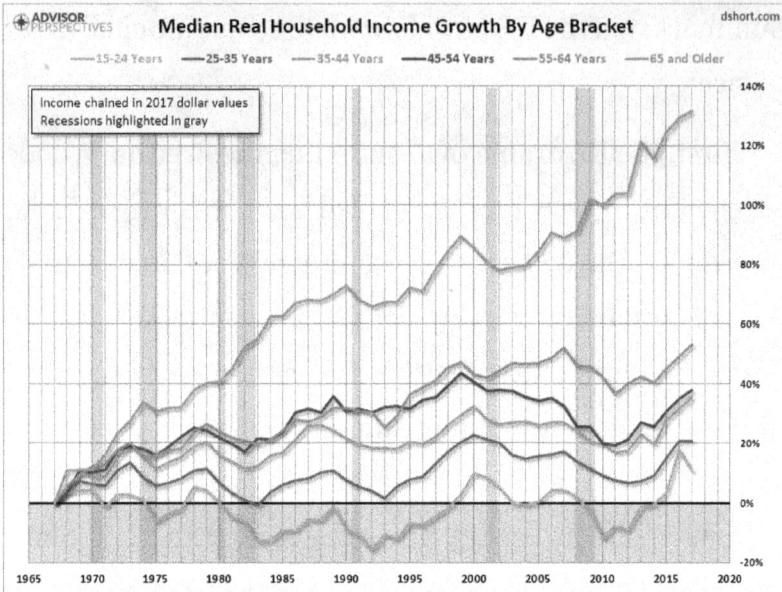

Figure 3.5: inflation-adjusted household incomes by age bracket.[28]

The last two huge economic problems are the issues of female retribution and youngsters' education. I will address these two topics in the next section.

3.3 Why Does Motherly Care Care?

Even though women are empathy-hardwired for child protection, one should not confuse brain wiring with

---

28 dhsort.com, Advisor Perspectives

human thinking nor acting. I explain this at length in a book called "deism versus theism", and the story is too long to repeat it in this pamphlet. Summarizing the conclusion: the difference between the two is the human spirit, source of free will.

Hence, women can understand and act in the spirit of Machiavelli, in much the same way as men can. There are many proofs around, the best-known ones being Queen Isabelle of Castile and Aragón, and English Prime Minister Margaret Thatcher, also known as the Iron Lady.[29] These two ladies alone are enough of a proof that women are able to think and act in terms of power. Hence, milady's, feminist or not, you have no excuse to desert.

As for the human species, she is way too young to allow for any significant genetic mutations as a consequence of social roles. Hence, whereas the muscle differences between sexes date from hundreds of millions of years, and social behavior due to muscles is therefore hardwired in our genes, abstract thinking is too recent a development to have left genetic traces. Yet, men have the social tradition to study the mechanisms of power, like

----

29 I do not at all think of these two very gifted ladies as female role models, though, but I do appreciate them both a lot.

our dangerous friend Niccolò. That is the only reason they are better educated in Machiavellism than women.

So how can we make women as rich as men? There is only one possible first step, and that is to deal with motherhood. To puke like Pavlov's dog when the term "mother" is mentioned, might be a very trendy and feminist thing to do, but it is merely a manifestation of stupidity.

Next you might ask: why should we deal with motherhood, as our ideal is the very opposite, to wit, to free ourselves from the traditional gender roles in society?

First, the richer a country, the more women freely choose for motherhood. I beg your pardon for my putting it so bluntly: this is a plain economical fact, not an issue of debate.

Second, in case motherhood were the very opposite of feminism, even feminists should learn to think strategically, like Machiavelli. One starts building one's house by the foundations. Then come the walls, and only finally the roof. We are now building the house, which symbolizes the tools or means by which we can get to our goals. Whatever those goals might be: pro-life, pro-separation, or pro-LGBT, I do not mind. Shouting out loud one's ideals is not only useless, it is even harmful to yourselves. You think not? Just grab whatever history book from the shelf, and you will read the confirmation that all winning strategies have been planned secretly. Hence, begin by building your pedestal and your social status: that is the "house". Your ideals are the paintings that you will decorate your house with: pornography, violence, rapes, or family pictures, whatever: every woman is free to choose. Just remember you cannot decorate a house that is not yet built.

A third social observation is that presently most happy families consist of husband, wife and children obtained naturally and within wedlock. I do not claim that those ingredients warrant happiness, nor that without those ingredients happiness is impossible. Neither do I claim these ingredients will never change: there might be some far future where the most happy families consist of two daddies, three mums, and four other primates with laboratory-begotten little primates.[30] But if you want changes now, you have to accept the social facts as they are now. By definition, the present facts do not correspond to feminist ideals. All the feminist anger displayed on television is simply due to the frustration in

---

30 Sooner or later, some dirty laboratory will manage to produce a kind of mixed species: cursed be they

experiencing that, whatever feminists try to do, nothing succeeds.

Anno 2019 the societal fact is that an appreciable amount of the female electorate wants to live traditional motherhood, that is, backed by a faithful husband. Instead of despising these women, why not politically use them for your purposes? When you understand this, you have reached the minimal level needed to assist to Machiavelli's classes. Let us begin our Machiavellian thinking by supposing that the percentage of women, choosing for traditional motherhood, does not change appreciably on short term.[31]

As strange as it might seem, the most efficient way to get an equal social status for men and women is to pay mothers for their motherly work. Note that I am not suggesting that mothers should not have a job outside: I am only claiming that, just like lawyers, bankers, businessmen, or politicians serve society by delivering a taxable product, mothers serve society by delivering future tax payers. Hence, they deserve[32] to be paid for

---

31 Anyway, changing that percentage is not your primary objective, neither immediate nor mediate, but a possible secondary objective. It is not about the paintings hanging on your walls, but about their frames.
32 by natural right

their service to society, like all people spending their time on jobs "outside".[33] Now, I do understand this sounds horribly anti-feminist, but Machiavelli is not about giving oneself a good feeling, but about gathering enough power (by deceit and false appearances if needed) to realize your goals.

Since the mothers' services to society consist in educating future tax-payers, the taxation authority is responsible for the mothers' salary and pension. Given that a society only thrives when financial retribution is quality-based, Machiavelli's proposal is the following:

- Every legally married mother earns a salary proportional to her children's grades at school, whatever the intellectual level of that school.[34]

- Every legally married mother receives a pension proportional to the taxes her

---

33 What philosopher is able to defend that time spent on serving society is more worthy outside than inside one's house?

34 be it a university or a school for heavily disabled children (syndrome of Down and the like)

children's families pay, standardized on the average taxes paid in their line of work.[35]

- These retributions (both salary and pension) diminish when the mother files for divorce, without evidence of her husband's misconduct.

The logical consequence of such a law is that

- the number of psychologically unstable people diminishes

- the number of divorces and duped children diminishes

- the number of women seeking a job outside diminishes

- the salaries for non-mother women rises

---

[35] The correction is such that a banker child who pays the average bankers' taxes, contributes equally to mother's pension as a cleaner's child who pays the average cleaner's taxes.

- women who choose so, can access all levels of responsibilities, as long as they are willing to sign a non-pregnancy contract

---

The most important power issue is that all women benefit from this proposal: LGBT, hetero, full-time mothers, part-time mothers, married mothers, divorced mothers, and non-mothers. That means, at least 50% of the total electorate! This fight is therefore impossible to lose for women. It is just a matter of endlessly explaining why the mother-retribution proposal is not anti-feminist, nor anti-male, but merely pro-justice.

CHAPTER 4
Boss in own Belly

4.1 Abortion

Everybody is boss in own belly. It is a silly slogan. What nobody can claim, however, is to be Master and Commander of whatever other human being. Consequently, abortion is, in ethical terms, a vomiting (because on one's own child) form of premeditated murder.

We all make our mistakes. So do not take a general ethical principle as a personal attack. If a friend of mine decided to have an abortion, that would not in the least affect our friendship. The most important reason is, quite simply, that I am not able to look into people's hearts. So who am I to judge?

Ratio	Reason for Abortion
<0.5%	Victim of rape
3%	Fetal health problems
4%	Physical health problems
4%	Would interfere with education or career
7%	Not mature enough to raise a child
8%	Don't want to be a single mother
19%	Done having children
23%	Can't afford a baby
25%	Not ready for a child
6%	Other

Table 4.1 Guttmacher Institute's anonymous survey of 1200 women

This being said, let us see for what reasons couples or single mothers choose for abortion. In 2004, the Guttmacher Institute anonymously surveyed 1,209 post-abortive women from nine different abortion clinics across the country. Of the women surveyed, 957 provided a main reason for having an abortion. Table 4.1 lists each reason and the percentage of respondents who chose it.

The world-wide reason to introduce legal abortion in the 1970's was to alleviate victims of rape. Since this number is vanishingly small, it follows directly that the introduction of abortion was planned by a mafia with world-wide reach. Given the nature and goals of EZ, I think it is quite obvious who financed it.

Apart from the 7% health-related reasons, 93% of the abortions are done for gravely insufficient reasons, that should be punishable by law like any other crime. Although this seems an anti-feminist law, it only protects women from pressure of their gullible boy friends.

4.2 The boyfriend's pressure does not appear in Guttmacher's table

Doesn't this contradict my previous statements concerning my not judging aborting mothers? I think not. I simply do not judge any mother of behaving well or not. However, I do believe the state or nation should have clear laws protecting society. In the case of abortion, it should be considered a crime. The main wrongdoer is usually the boyfriend alias sperm donor, and the second one the poor mother. In fact, many aborting mothers are psychologically too confused about themselves, to even mention their friend's pressure, whether outspoken or implicit. Would none of the Guttmacher categories contain some of that pressure? Of course. As a matter of fact, apart from the first four categories, I would consider all others as due to that pressure. *And they represent 89% of all abortions.*

So wat are we looking at? At nothing but female inferiority with respect to men. Men want to have sex with no risks and no long-term relations. The large majority of men apparently only want sex with girls who accept being treated like fuckable throw-away beer cans. This is the very definition of male sexual addiction, and female submission.[36]

4.3 The case of Abby Johnson

In her book "The Walls are Talking", she writes:

> When the nation's largest abortion provider claimed that abortion represented only 3% of the services

---

36 Equally submissive was Dutch hard-core feminist Heleen Mees' proposal to suck Buiter's balls. I have no idea what makes people think that Heleen Mees is feminist. The very facts point out that she does nothing to improve the status of women. What she does, is offering herself as a throw-away whore. Once she did what she had wanted to, she suddenly feels humiliated, and dedicates all her life to ruin Willem Buiter.

provided, I doggedly embraced that "fact". The longer I was a part of the industry and the deeper I delved into the inner workings of the clinic, both medical and financial, even I found that fact impossible to believe. I knew what brought women to our clinic, and I knew exactly what "services" we were providing. The numbers simply didn't add up. When I went to my supervisors about this, I was instantly shot down. Instead of brainstorming with me about ways to reduce abortions, they talked of budgets and the need to increase our cash flow. The way we did that? Abortion.

As Johnson discovered, abortion was a mere money-maker for Planned Parenthood. Planned Parenthood uses manipulative tactics during abortion counseling, lying about fetal development, until using outright coercion. Abby Johnson converted a pro-lifer after having seen the abortion of a 13-week-old preborn baby on ultrasound. She now uses the insider knowledge she gained by working for Planned Parenthood to fight the abortion industry. For that purpose, she founded "And Then There Were None", an organization which dissuades abortion workers to continue working in the abortion business. At the 44th annual March for Life she said "I believe that in the next four years we will see the end of Roe vs Wade". She was accompanied on stage by 12 fellow abortion industry "quitters." They were, she said, only a

small percentage of the 330 former abortion employees
that had been rescued by "And Then There Were None".

4.4 Technical Mistakes

John Jalsevac published in 2010 on LifeSiteNews.com the
following communication:

> A recent study by the Environmental Protection
> Agency (EPA) has confirmed 1988 as a "change point"
> in the rise of Autism Disorder rates in the U.S. - a
> date that pro-life leaders say correlates with the
> introduction of fetal cells for use in vaccines. While
> the EPA study does not speculate into the cause of
> the jump in autism rates, and makes no mention of
> aborted fetal cells, the researchers point out that it
> "is important to determine whether a preventable
> exposure to an environmental factor may be
> associated with the increase." According to the pro-
> life group Sound Choice Pharmaceutical Institute
> (SCPI), which specializes in vaccine research, that
> "environmental factor" may well be the use of aborted
> fetal cells in vaccines. The group pointed out in its
> most recent newsletter that 1988 is the same year
> the U.S. Advisory Committee on Immunization
> Practices began recommending a second dose of the
> MMR vaccine, which included cells derived from the
> tissue of aborted babies. Analyses of autism rate data
> published by SCPI identify 3 clear change points in
> U.S. autism disorder trends: 1981, 1988 and 1995, all
> of which the group claims roughly correlate with the

use of vaccines (Meruvax, MMRII, and Chickenpox) that were cultivated with the use of tissue from aborted children. The group says that it has been unable to identify any other factor that might correlate to the change in autism rates. "The only environmental event correlating with these statistical autism trend 'change points' which would impact almost all children was the introduction of vaccines produced using human fetal cells and containing residual human DNA and cellular debris," said SCPI. Pro-life groups say that the research by EPA adds to an increasing body of evidence implicating the use of aborted fetal cell material in the nationwide vaccinations impacting nearly every child born in the United States. American Life League has joined Sound Choice Pharmaceutical Institute in calling for a Fair Labeling and Informed Consent Act in light of the findings. "For years the evidence has pointed toward the link between vaccines using DNA from aborted babies and the rise of Autism Disorder rates," said Jim Sedlak, vice president of American Life League. "Parents need and deserve to know the risks associated with vaccinations made from lines derived from the bodies of aborted children." SCPI has affirmed that they are continuing to study the impact of residual human fetal DNA in vaccines on the brain development and autism in children, and will present their studies at the International Society for Autism Research in May 2010.

4.5 Clearing addictions

The damage caused by sexual addiction is colossal. EZ knows this and promotes everything that can possibly degrade societies (except their own patriarchal one, of course: ever seen Mrs. or Ms. Rothschild publicly take a political initiative?). That is the long term idea of EZ: at some future time, the only healthy society will be EZ's, and all others will be enslaved by addictions. Whatever still walks around loose, will do so in shackles and serve the superior race.

Since going to war presently is a granted suicide (as all arms and military units are already in their hands), a society has to protect herself from EZ by actively fighting addictions. Adios, Las Vegas. Put the whole thing in a garbage can. Adios, brothels, every guy caught on a tape goes straight to prison. Adios, street whores, you go all straight to prison, together with the guy that invites you in his car. Adios, parents who do not teach their youngsters to curb their sexual desires, their addictions to movies or to games: you will lose mother's wage and pension because your children will underperform at school.

I would not recommend to spend money on addicted adults, who lack the motivation to get clean. They have no cure. The only way to win the battle is that youngsters never even come close to an addictive temptation. And yes, of course, criminals who induce youngsters to whatever addition (drugs, sex, games, etc.) should be *hanged on the spot*, after a high-priority trial. The only way they could save their lives should be by providing proof of bigger dealers, which will then be hanged in their place.

Once this policy starts bearing fruit, government might have some time left to meddle with the number of selected garbage containers, the severity of tickets for parking on the wrong spot, and other highly irrelevant issues.

Summarizing, the whole boss-in-own-belly movement is EZ-initiated, EZ-financed and EZ-promoted. It addicts males to cheap sex and it lowers women to the status of whores. No free person (male or female) in her right mind can ever like it.

CHAPTER 5
A Retrograde Parental Attitude

5.1 Lifting the ban on separate education

The ban on separate-sex high-schools is purely ideological, highly detrimental to young girls, and a grave extremist intromission in the freedom of families to decide whatever education they want for their children. Lefties have their mouth full of tolerance toward other people (trans genders and the like), but they suddenly turn into dictators when separate education is concerned. Lefties have a pathologically distorted self-perception: they really believe they are tolerant. Once left and right was about income or belief. Today leftism is a combination of intolerance, unethicality, hypocrisy, political manipulation, and solipsism.

Now please tell me, leftie, what could possibly wrong with separate education? I mean, what fundamental rights are we trampling on here? The facts are that separate education takes away the social roles. Is that not what feminism was after?

Separated education takes away the male tendency to show off a chick harem, whether by means of sending some competitor class mates to hospital or not. It takes away the female competition for being the most attractive girl, if needed, by organizing a full-isolation attack on her competitor. It takes away the fear, for males, to choose a "typical female education", like one based on esthetics (e.g. dancing, or beauty diving). It takes away the fear, for females, to choose a "typical male education", like engineering or mathematics.

The following quote is from "The High School for Girls":[37]

> The High School for Girls has a national reputation for academic excellence. Outstanding results are achieved not only through our students gaining the top A* and A grades, but with the progress that every student makes during their time at the High School. This pursuit of educational success consistently makes the High School for Girls one of the top state schools in the country. In the summer of 2016 High School Sixth Form students achieved their best ever

37 https://www.hsfg.org/page/?title=Performance&pid=11

results in the top grades. The proportion of qualifications at A*-B rose significantly from 67% in 2015 to 76.1% in 2016, testimony to the dedication, enthusiasm and hard work of both staff and students.[38]

Take a look at the two pictures below. Something wrong with femininity here? Look at the exquisite feminine empathic expression of the girl on the left, and at the carefully polished nails of the girl at the right (separate education is compatible with going out at night). These are our future high-profile directives!

---

38 In the national context of falling numbers of A*-A grades being achieved at A-Level, the percentage of qualifications at these grades increased from 36.3% to 41.6%. The High School Sixth Form students achieved above the national average of A* grades. Individual students had fantastic success. Over a fifth of the cohort achieved at least 3 As in all three of their A2 qualifications. Students have secured their places on their chosen courses including Oxbridge, Russell Group of universities, Music Colleges and on Art Foundation courses. In addition to the outstanding results at the top end, 93.3% of all qualifications were graded at least C or above with the overall pass mark at A-Level at 100%. Our GCSE students also celebrated success in the summer of 2016. The High School's commitment to enable all students to believe, achieve and thrive and the outstanding work ethic of our students delivered another year of outstanding results. Over 70% of all GCSEs taken were graded at A or A*. Students at the High School continue to make excellent progress from their starting points entering the school. This was particularly noticeable in the number of the top grades achieved with over a quarter of all GCSEs being awarded at A*. Our outstanding results are just one reason why we have been rated the second best, state-funded secondary school in Gloucestershire. See 'The Real School Guide for Gloucestershire 2016'.

Deep concentration and a School Uniform. The latter eliminates all exhibitions of personal wealth and is a just as effective as cheap a passive educational element.

5.2 The more feminist the mother, the more conventional (anti-feminist) her education

The urgent problem with female minorities in scientific disciplines is due to parents' retrograde gender concepts and expectations. Parents show off their belief in the cause of feminism, whenever the rights of their daughters are in discussion. "If my daughter (of 15 years) chooses to have sex with her teacher (of 50 years), is that *our* business? Should we not leave *her* the freedom to decide?" This is not even an ironic view on feminism, it is straight irresponsible and immoral mistreatment. Would you have your children walk in a pharmacy and let them take whatever medication, because of the nice colors and smells?

German research produced the following numbers concerning parents' expectations that their daughters will ever study typical boys' stuff, like Mathematics, Informatics, Natural Science, or Technology (MINT in German), with the explicit goal of pursuing a MINT-career:

ELTERN SEHEN TÖCHTER NICHT IN EINER MINT-KARRIERE*
Anteil der Schüler, deren Eltern erwarten, dass sie einmal in MINT-Berufen arbeiten werden
in Prozent

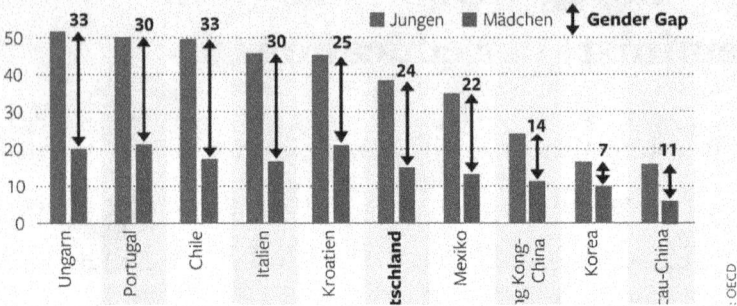

Figure 5.1 Parents' expectations of their daughters pursuing a MINT-career.[39]

The countries are, in order of appearance: Hungary, Portugal, Chile, Italy, Croatia, Germany, Mexico, Hong Kong, South Korea, and Macao. Boys are represented by the blue, girls by the red columns. Curiously, Italian expectations are among the most traditional, while in reality their percentage of female MINT professors is higher than average in Europe.

Well, my dear retrograde parents, when will you open your eyes, and stop throwing your daughters to the lions, in the name of an imbecile interpretation of feminism? Possibly *your* daughter does not spend a minute on

---

39 Infografik Die Welt, quoted in a contribution by Tanja Tricarico (March 2015)

homework for school, but word-wide the statistics indicate that girls daily spend 20 to 30% more time on homework than boys. If your daughter does not fit in these statistics, she must suffer some pathology, or you are unethically underperforming as her educators. Oh yes, and try to be a bit more feminist. Expecting your daughter to marry a smart, good-looking, rich boy, and teach her the tricks to catch him by surprise, is an antifeminist, quasi-retarded female education model.[40] What a teen-age girl needs to know of boys, basically reduces to these two points:

- boys act like predators, and compete for the highest number of girls they manage to penetrate; having sex has nothing whatsoever in common with loving a girl;

- it is possible to "educate" a boy in gallantry and monogamy, and to teach him to curb his sexual desires in order to grow in love. Love is a matter of sacrifice, not of penetration.

---

40 In classical patriarchal societies like the ancient Roman, Greek, Jewish, Persian, Native American, African, Asian and Australian, women were thought of as a weaker and dumber variant of men, fit only for educating children.

Parents who do not understand these two points, or fail to teach them properly to their daughters, can be sure that their genes will soon go extinct. So dear parents, do society a favor and sharpen your course, for the good of society as a whole. We will grant you a Darwin's award.

5.3 Marriage and divorce

The two graphs below illustrate the difference between a healthy and a sick society.

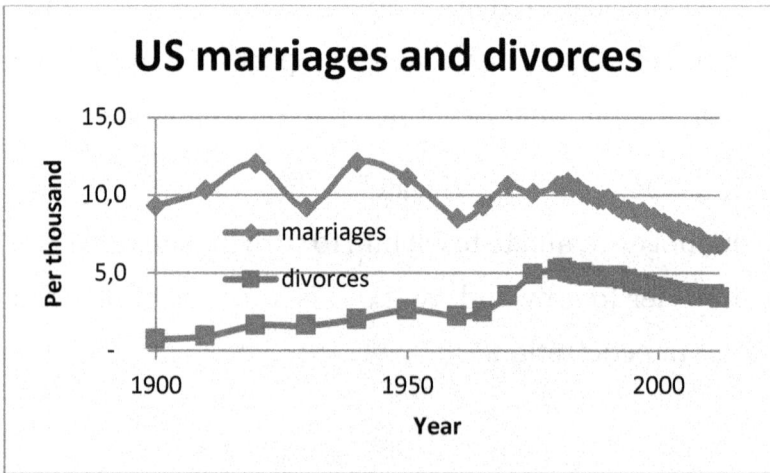

Figure 5.2: Marriages and divorces

per thousand pairs per year.

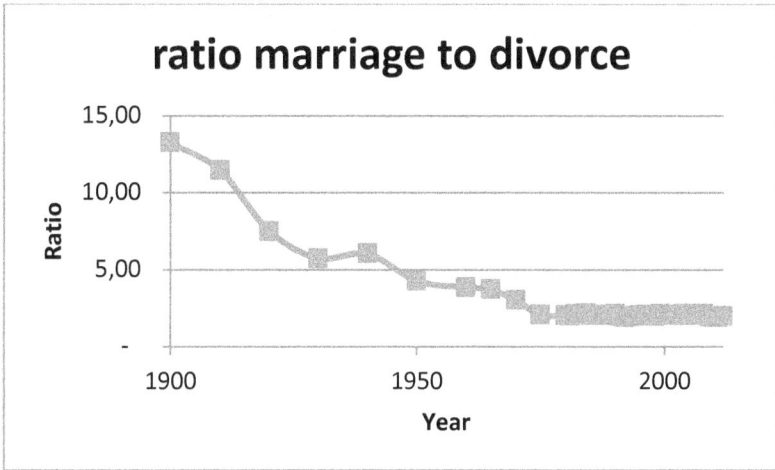

Figure 5.3: The ratio of marriages over divorces in the US, from 1900 to 2012.

As nothing changes in the marriage-divorce ratio beyond the sexual revolution (which supposed a lethal blow for the population-relative number of marriages), one may safely suppose that today we still witness half our marriages ending up in a divorce. In 1900, when the concept of "chastity" had any meaning at all, the ratio was already steeply falling. The enlightenment did an excellent job, again. I would not be surprised that in the so-called "dark ages" people were so virtuously illuminated that their ratio was beyond 100.[41] By the way,

----

41 "Of course", the deist will reply. "That was because women were treated as slaves!" Well, that is a phenomenal opinion. What was the percentage of whores in the dark ages? A factor 100 less

witch-trials were introduced by the Enlightenment, and strongly opposed by the Catholic Church. Voltaire and his lying followers managed to convince the largely acritical population[42] of the opposite. Both (the lack of criticality, and the completely wrong conception of history) are a majority phenomenon today.

5.4 The Smartphone

Even in healthy marriages, parents often have not sufficient comprehension of children's mental world to correctly judge the way smartphones should be used. Since in general women are more sensible to this problematic than men, the present book seemed to me a good context to mention a few basic, common sense ideas, which moreover have been confirmed by smart psychological studies. The most comprehensible example is that where parents pick up their children from school. It makes quite a lot of difference if mum or dad are

---

than today, no doubt. Too bad there are no statistics about them. But it is difficult to imagine a society in which almost all women are married either to men or to God, to also have a large percentage of whores.

42 I mean, those who believe everything written and said in the media.

looking at the school exit, and wave at their child leaving school, versus the same mum or dad saying "hi darling" when their child steps into the car, with mum or dad busy with their smartphones. In the first case the children feel loved by the parents, in the second case they feel like second-order to their parents' smartphones. Who does not understand this, can simply skip the rest of the section.

5.4.1. Tristan Harris

The below text is taken from Harris' own homepage.[43]

> Called the "closest thing Silicon Valley has to a conscience," by The Atlantic magazine, Tristan Harris spent three years as a Google Design Ethicist developing a framework for how technology should "ethically" steer the thoughts and actions of billions of people from screens. He is now co-founder of the Center for Humane Technology, whose mission is to reverse 'human downgrading' and re-align technology with humanity.
>
> Rolling Stone magazine named Tristan one of "25 People Shaping the World", and was named in Fortune's 40 under 40 of 2018 for his work on reforming technology. In 2016, Tristan left Google to work on reforming the attention economy with the non-profit initiative, Time Well Spent which called out

---

43 https://www.tristanharris.com/#!

the industry's "race to the bottom of the brain stem" to capture attention and proposed design solutions. In January 2018, Mark Zuckerberg embraced "time well spent" as a design goal for Facebook, and in May 2018, Apple and Google each launched "Digital Wellbeing" initiatives and "time well spent" features now shipping on iOS and Android phones.

Tristan has spent more than a decade studying the influences that hijack human thinking and action. From his childhood as a magician to his work in the Stanford Persuasive Technology Lab where he studied persuasive technology, Tristan became concerned about the need for ethical and humane technology.

A year after his company was acquired by Google in 2013, he created an internal slide deck within Google that went viral, warning about technology's arms race to capture attention and the moral responsibility of technology companies in how they shape society.

Tristan's work has been featured on TED,[44] 60 Minutes, HBO RealTime with Bill Maher, PBS NewsHour, Recode, The Atlantic, WIRED, NYTimes, Der Spiegel, The Economist, and many more. Tristan has briefed Heads of State, technology company CEOs, and members of U.S. Congress about the attention economy. He is a senior fellow at Common Sense Media, and an advisor to the Open Markets Institute.

Before Google, Tristan was co-founder and CEO of Apture, which Google acquired in 2011. Apture

---

44 https://www.ted.com/talks/tristan_harris_the_
    manipulative_tricks_tech_companies_use_to_capture_your_
    attention

enabled millions of users to get instant, on-the-fly explanations across a vast publisher network.

Tristan holds several patents from his work at Apple, Wikia, Apture and Google. He graduated from Stanford University with a degree in Computer Science, focused on Human Computer Interaction, while dabbling in behavioral economics, social psychology, behavior change and habit formation in Professor BJ Fogg's Stanford Persuasive Technology lab.

5.4.2. Sherry Turkle

The below text is taken from the sternspeaker website.[45]

The world is finally catching up to Sherry Turkle. For more than three decades, the MIT professor and New York Times best-selling author has warned that technology is undermining human empathy. Her research has demonstrated how screen technology tried to do one thing: keep us at our screens—compromising our capacity for solitude, a building block for identity and the ability to form relationships. And technology encourages the idea that the "friction-free" life is the good life. Turkle's research shows how in business, education, and personal spheres, the value of friction-free existence has been over-rated, even destructive. Technology, Turkle has shown, makes us forget what we know

---

45 https://sternspeakers.com/speakers/sherry-turkle/

about life.

In life, when we stumble and lose our words in face-to-face conversation, it can be painful, but we reveal ourselves most to each other. Online, we can make ourselves appear closer to our ideal selves than we know ourselves to be. Online, we preach authenticity but practice self-curation. We learn to fear vulnerability. But it turns out that vulnerability is what makes us human, productive, empathic and creative, in our personal and professional lives.

Now, with popular optimism about all things tech turning to wariness and hostility, Turkle's groundbreaking work is prescient and addresses our most current dilemmas. Most to the point: As organizations embrace artificial intelligence, they will have to grapple with an existential question that Turkle strives to address: how can we still be most truly human in the age of machines?

As a sociologist and psychologist, Professor Turkle's exploration of our lives on the digital terrain shows how technological advancement doesn't just catalyze changes in what we do – it affects how we think. She has documented how in our embrace of convenience, we have shielded ourselves from having to converse and cooperate with other human beings. Turkle is the original and still leading expert on how these trends impact our social skills and emotional intelligence. Her keynotes and presentations aim to shift the way organizations and society think about technology – from an emphasis on convenience and simplification to an embrace of the messy, complex reality of how humans learn and become better people. Turkle's research also raises critical questions about technology's role in business productivity, asking whether multi-tasking actually leads to deteriorating performance in each of our tasks.

Referred to by many as the "Margaret Mead of digital culture," Professor Turkle has investigated the intersection of digital technology and human relationships from the early days of personal computers to our current world of robotics, AI, social networking and mobile connectivity. Her New York Times best-seller, "Reclaiming Conversation: The Power of Talk in a Digital Age" (Penguin Press, October 2015), focuses on the importance of conversation in digital cultures, including business, the professions and in education. Her previous book, "Alone Together: Why We Expect More from Technology and Less from Each Other" (Basic Books, 2011), was a featured talk at TED 2012, describing technology's influence on relationships between friends, lovers, parents and children, and new instabilities in how we understand privacy and community, intimacy and solitude.[46]

Professor Turkle is the Abby Rockefeller Mauzé Professor of the Social Studies of Science and Technology in the Program in Science, Technology and Society at MIT, as well as the founding director of Initiative on Technology and Self, a center of research and reflection on the evolving connections between people and artifacts. She has been profiled in such publications as The New York Times, Scientific American and WIRED. She is a featured media commentator on the effects of technology for CNN, NBC, ABC and NPR, including appearances on

---

46 https://www.ted.com/talks/sherry_turkle_alone_together

such programs as Nightline, 20/20 and The Colbert Report, and has been named a Harvard Centennial Medalist, and a Ms. Magazine Woman of the Year. In 2014, she was named to the American Academy of Arts and Sciences, and in 2017, she received the Everett M. Rogers Award from the Norman Lear Center at USC Annenberg.

Professor Turkle received a joint doctorate in sociology and personality psychology from Harvard University, and is a licensed clinical psychologist.

5.4.3. Nancy Jo Sales

The text below is taken from Nancy Jo's own website.[47]

Nancy Jo Sales is a New York Times bestselling author and award-winning journalist who has written for Vanity Fair and many other publications. Known for her stories on youth culture, celebrity culture, and social media, Nancy Jo is also a filmmaker. Her HBO documentary, SWIPED: HOOKING UP IN THE DIGITAL AGE (2018), is an investigation into how technology has changed the landscape of sex and dating. Her book American Girls: Social Media and the Secret Lives of Teenagers (2016)[48] explores how social media has transformed the lives of girls and young women and presented them with unprecedented challenges, especially the scourge of online sexism. Her book The Bling Ring: How A Gang of Fame-

---

47 http://www.nancyjosales.com/bio/
48 https://www.nytimes.com/2016/03/27/books/review/
   american-girls-by-nancy-jo-sales.html

Obsessed Teens Ripped Off Hollywood and Shocked the World (2013) tells the true story behind the Sofia Coppola film The Bling Ring (2013), which was based on Nancy Jo's Vanity Fair piece, "The Suspects Wore Louboutins." Born in West Palm Beach, Florida, Nancy Jo attended the Phillips Exeter Academy, graduating as a Presidential Scholar. She was a summa cum laude, Phi Beta Kappa graduate of Yale, which awarded her its Willet's Prize for fiction writing. She received her MFA in Writing from Columbia University in 1991. Her awards include a 2011 Front Page Award for Best Magazine Feature and a 2010 Mirror Award for Best Profile, Digital Media.

5.4.4. Walter Mischel

The text below is taken from Wikipedia.[49]

The Stanford marshmallow experiment was a series of studies on delayed gratification in the late 1960s and early 1970s led by psychologist Walter Mischel, then a professor at Stanford University. In these studies, a child was offered a choice between one small reward provided immediately or two small rewards if they waited for a short period, approximately 15 minutes, during which the tester left the room and then returned. (The reward was sometimes a marshmallow, but often a cookie or a pretzel.) In follow-up studies, the researchers found

---

49 https://en.wikipedia.org/wiki/Stanford_
    marshmallow_experiment

that children who were able to wait longer for the preferred rewards tended to have better life outcomes, as measured by SAT scores, educational attainment, body mass index (BMI), and other life measures.

5.4.5. Christof Van Nimwegen

Van Nimwegen is a Dutch scientist, working at Utrecht University.[50] Below follows the Conclusive section of his 2006 scientific paper[51]

"The Paradox of the Assisted User: Guidance can be Counterproductive"

by Van Nimwegen, Burgos, Van Oostendorp, and Schijf.

In this booklet we do not reproduce the references; they can be found in the paper itself.

This research investigated the influences that interface style and cognitive style have on planful behavior from the user and consequently on problem solving performance. These issues are beyond plain usability issues, and instead we focus on more (meta) cognitive aspects of interface-induced behavior, namely planfulness and user engagement. Our first hypothesis stating that internalization leads to more planning and better performance than externalization

---

50 https://www.academia.edu/19549508/
    The_paradox_of_the_assisted_user
51 CHI (2006) April 22–28

is supported both by time-based and move-based measures. As in earlier experiments [21, 21, 22], it once again showed that (now also in this more realistic task) user behavior differed depending on interface style. The time-based measures showed that the interface style requiring (more) internalization resulted in longer thinking times before subjects started working on the problem, and also more time between moves, which we took as indicators of planning. Both these results indicate that when information has to be internalized, more contemplation from the user is provoked. This is in line with results of O'Hara and Payne [13], who reported a longer inter-move latency for subjects in the effortful condition, indicating a more plan-based approach. Also interesting are the conclusions that can be drawn from the move-based measures. It has to be born in mind that the issue here was not "can they solve it?" but "how smart or efficiently do they solve it?", since in the end each problem had a solution, and these tasks are not extremely difficult given the limited number of speakers. Results showed that internalization subjects solved the problems with fewer superfluous moves, in a more straightforward manner, thus with less deviation from the minimum amount of moves, resulting in greater efficiency. We infer that the shorter solution paths are a result stemming from better planning. These superfluous moves included "correction moves", moves made to "repair" situations that sometimes were created by users making "not so smart" moves. Superfluous moves also included "reconsidered moves" (when a user started a move but changed his mind and puts it back, like a chess player who realizes his mistake a fraction after he picks up a piece). These findings converge with our earlier results [20, 21, 22] in which there were strong tendencies in that direction. The results are also in line with O'Hara and Payne [13, 14] who found that the subjects with a plan- based approach used fewer moves than subjects using a display-based approach. They also stated that "backtracking" (undoing a move and return to previous situation) occurred more in subjects showing display-based problem solving. In sum, although there was no significant difference in the total time taken to complete the tasks, there were differences in how efficient, in which manner subjects solve the problems. All subjects needed about the same total amount of time, but subjects who were required to internalize thought longer before moves and came up with more efficient solutions. This converges with results from other research [7, 13, 14, 20, 21, 22]. The results reflect a trade-off between time spent thinking and planning (internalization subjects) and time spent making superfluous moves (externalization subjects). The fact that internalization subjects came out of the experiment with better declarative knowledge strengthens our interpretation that these subjects spend the extra thinking time on planning and learning. All this might be of value in for example a transfer task, or when doing a similar task after a big lapse of time. This interpretation also gets some support from internalization subjects' tendency to use a more appropriate strategy. Regarding the strategy that subjects chose to use, a qualitative analysis of the results pointed at a more plan- based approach by the internalization subjects, showing that those subjects more often filled the timetable by first scheduling speakers with the most constraints. This strategy is again an indicator of good planning, because it shows that people think about whom, and how they are going to schedule before starting with the task. The issue of strategy use could merit more interest in future research. Also, it would be interesting to investigate whether subjects stick to the same strategy or change it, if they feel it is unproductive or if another less effortful strategy suffices. Another interesting question would be whether strategy choice can be influenced (e.g., by providing feedback, or externalizing strategy support, as mentioned in [16]). The second hypothesis has to be rejected. Cognitive style, at least along our dimension of high NFC versus low NFC had no influence; pre-existing attitudes towards problem solving did not have significant effects on the displayed behavior and performance of subjects. Perhaps the strong effects of interface style overruled possible effects of pre- existing individual differences in cognitive style. However, the lack of findings may also be due to our subjects' high NFC scores. The difference in scores between high-NFC and low-NFC may not have been large enough to produce significant results. Another possible reason for the lack of findings is that our task might have been too easy for the subjects, not needing the extra impetus from having high NFC-scores. This is supported by answers in the post experimental questionnaire concerning the perceived difficulty. Subjects reported having little difficulty with the tasks, and the cognitive effort required was quite low. We also tested the knowledge subjects possessed after completing the tasks. In the declarative knowledge questions, subjects had to judge situations where the rules sometimes were violated. They had to identify whether the shown situations were theoretically possible or not. They had to look at the constraints of a situation, and decide whether any "rule" was violated (such as a speaker with an audience of 120 placed in a room where only 75 fitted). The expected effect of interface style on declarative knowledge questions was almost significant, although not as strong as in earlier experiments with B&B [20, 21, 22]. It showed that internalization subjects tended to give more correct answers to those questions. An explanation for the better answers by internalization subjects could be the fact that in all the tasks before, they proved to have thought and planned more. Perhaps a training effect occurred that made them more accurate on these questions too. There were also several procedural knowledge questions. These were not so much about judgment, but about insight on what to do to solve a part of a problem. As expected, interface style had no effect here, no differences concerning answers to the procedural questions were found (performance was nearly at ceiling). In a way this is not very surprising, since the problems were not so difficult, and we also saw that all subjects correctly solved al the situations. This pattern is similar to the one found in previous experiments: a positive effect of internalization on declarative knowledge, and no effect on procedural knowledge [20, 21, 22]. Lastly, the opinion questions indicated that all the subjects had little difficulty performing the tasks and were confident about their own performance. There were hardly any differences between the two interface styles, although the scores of internalization subjects were marginally higher. One question yielded significantly different scores, pointing at an advantage of internalization. We asked whether the subjects sometimes did not know how to proceed with the arrangement of the speakers. This "feeling stuck" occurred significantly more often in the externalization condition than in the internalization condition. This lends support to the finding that externalization subjects needed more superfluous moves (they had to make corrections more often) to complete the tasks. We take this also as an indicator that the internalization subjects had better insight. To sum up our conclusions, at not any point or with any measure did externalization result in better performance, reconfirming various earlier findings. Also in a more realistic task, we found positive effects of internalization on problem-solving behavior: having the user internalize the information leads to a more plan-based behavior, smarter solution paths, better declarative knowledge, and less feeling lost. Externalization on the other hand led to a more display-based approach, resulting in less efficient solutions (more moves) and less thinking about moves to be made. It is worthwhile to reflect on what was in effect externalized and visualized. In the externalization condition this was the result of applying the set of constraints that was attached to the speaker, to the sets of constraints attached to the scheduling slots. The interface showed which actions are allowed with the object at hand. Subjects were able to see the outcome of the application of the rules. This is comparable to the graying out of menu items in for example Microsoft Word, showing that the current situation does not permit those functions to be used. We showed that this widely accepted and implemented guideline does sometimes have undesirable effects. In the real world, when designing interfaces we have to be careful with providing interface cues that give away too much, and must design in such a manner that the way users think is optimally supported. Interaction designers could consider making interactions for a user "more difficult", or better "less assisted" on purpose, to persuade users to adopt such specific behavior. This in turn could help the software to achieve its specific goal. How can we link all this to general aspects of usability such as learnability, satisfaction, errors/memorability and efficiency [12]? In previous research by the authors we saw that errors/memorability (especially memorability) was better in the internalization condition [20, 21]. Concerning errors, the current results concerning superfluous moves (although they are not the same as errors) point at an advantage for internalization. Efficiency in terms of "path economy" was better in the situations where subjects had to internalize information themselves. Satisfaction was not our main focus, but there was a question (question 6, Table 3) reflecting satisfaction, and there was no difference between the interfaces. We feel that understanding how people react to interface information (based on cognitive findings) is one of the main challenges in HCI research. Our research shows that a computer mediated task can take advantage of interfaces that are designed from considerations that run deeper than plain usability. With all kinds of multimedia present in all corners of society, our research contributes to building bridges between cognitive science, HCI and current educational practices. Our findings, especially if extended to even more realistic tasks can be valuable in the development of applications in the realm of education, multimedia learning or game based learning, and still others. Examples are interactive learning devices in museums that try to explain certain principles, but also more generally other situations where learning as good as possible or when certain issues are at stake, and making as little mistakes as possible or speed are important. There are of course situations in which the investigated issues are not crucial at all, but, depending on the specific goal and situation, designing software in such a way that active learning is being provoked can be valuable. We expect that having knowledge internalized can be important when dependence on the existence of a particular interface is specifically not desired, or when speeding up a task is important, just to name a few situations. One can think of situations where risky and complex tasks are performed, and where a user suddenly is required to a new situation. Now his/her insights and knowledge has to be transferred to a different situation. The common guideline to "not give users the chance to make mistakes" should of course not be neglected, but at the same time, interaction should facilitate or even persuade users to learn what underlies the task they are doing. The investigated concepts are important in situations where learning itself is the aim, but one can also think of situations where making errors generates a high cost. An example would be certain types of medical software, where it is important that users master underlying concepts at all times, and are continuously provoked to "actively think". Likewise, one can also think of process operators in for example a hydroelectric power plant. They use process control software that will assist and prevent errors, especially with crucial or difficult tasks. If the system would break down and operators have to manually do the job that is normally done aided by computers, will they still know what exactly underlies the task? Examples are actions that must be performed in a certain order, such as opening valves, closing a circuit and so on. Or are they so used to the information and feedback from the interface that they will now be stuck? In this light, Fu and Gray [9] found that when inefficient procedures are chosen to solve a problem, these procedures shared two characteristics. They are often generic and well-practiced, but more importantly the procedure is composed of interactive components that bring fast, incremental feedback on the external problem states. These actions require less cognitive effort, but this bias to depend on interactive units unfortunately leads to paths that require more effort in the long run. The title of this paper is of course a wink to the famous book chapter by Carroll and Rosson [5] entitled "The paradox of the active user". This term refers to a common observation that users never read manuals but start using software immediately. They are not very interested in the system, and don't want to spend time up front on getting established, or going through learning packages. It is a paradox because users would save time in the long run by taking some time to optimize the system and learn more about it. The paradox in our research would be that users that received an interface providing some assistance come up with less smart solutions, among other things. This assistance from the interface of course is meant to help, but appears to be counter effective. The conclusion of the two paradoxes could be the same: depending on the purpose of the software, we must perhaps design for the way users think and behave in reality.

5.4.6. Shalini Misra

Below we reproduce the complete abstract of the scientific paper "The iPhone Effect: The Quality of In-Person Social Interactions in the Presence of Mobile Devices", written by Misra, Cheng, Genevie, and Yuan, as a Research Article in *Environment and Behavior* (2014) July 1.[52]

This study examined the relationship between the presence of mobile devices and the quality of real-life in-person social interactions. In a naturalistic field experiment, 100 dyads were randomly assigned to discuss either a casual or meaningful topic together. A trained research assistant observed the participants unobtrusively from a distance during the course of a 10-min conversation noting whether either participant placed a mobile device on the table or held it in his or her hand. Using Hierarchical Linear Modeling, it was found that conversations in the absence of mobile communication technologies were rated as significantly superior compared with those in

---

52 https://doi.org/10.1177/0013916514539755

the presence of a mobile device, above and beyond the effects of age, gender, ethnicity, and mood. People who had conversations in the absence of mobile devices reported higher levels of empathetic concern. Participants conversing in the presence of a mobile device who also had a close relationship with each other reported lower levels of empathy compared with dyads who were less friendly with each other. Implications for the nature of social life in ubiquitous computing environments are discussed.

Appendix
Giorgia Meloni

Giorgia Meloni is the only female party leader in Italy. She has a son, her husband has left, and her party is called "Fratelli d'Italia" (brothers of Italy), which is directly quoted from the Italian national hymn. In other words, she strongly opposes all attempts to split Italy up in a rich northern part and a poor southern part. I believe her brains are S-wired, like those of Margaret Thatcher, Neelie Kroes, Jeanne d'Arc, and countless other women we never hear of. I also believe she understands what needs to happen in society, in order to reach the elusive *goal of gender equality with respect to social status.* This is not at all the feministic ideal, which is gender equality *in jobs and wages.* So let us hear Giorgia Meloni's political speech at the WCF (World Congress of Families) in Verona (Northern Italy), celebrated March 30, 2019.

Thank you! I just arrived. I was ironing. Then I found
ten minutes to come and talk about politics with you.
And I really think that this large presence here, [and]
outside, despite the many controversies surrounding
this initiative, this congress, is the best answer that
could be given. [...].

They scolded us for everything in the days
preceding this congress: They said that we are
retrograde, that we are *losers*, that we are
unpresentable, that we are *obscurantists*. They claim
it a scandal that someone wants to defend natural
family founded on marriage; to stimulate the birth
rate; to give the right value to human life; to support
educational freedom; to say "no!" to gender ideology.

These charges rather describe the sender.
Retrograde is someone who endeavors at bringing
censorship back to Italy by having our manifestation
annulled. *Obscurantist* is a State that, having
sponsored exhibitions that depicted a crucifix
immersed in a glass of pee, is ashamed to patronage a
World Congress of Family. *Loser* is whoever has little
else to do than to come here to insult us. Yes,
unpresentable are those who support the rented
womb; abortion at the ninth month; and denial of
medical treatment to eleven year olds!

They have said everything about this congress.
That we want to limit women's freedom. That we want
them at home cooking and ironing. Da ya see me home
i'ning?

Imagine me, the only female political party
secretary in Italy, me, a pregnant candidate for mayor
of Rome (I have been scolded for this), me advocating
for the relegation of women? Quite the contrary. I
aim at granting rights that don't even exist today. The

right for a woman to be a mother without having to give up her job. The right of a woman to be a mother and choose not to work, without dying a slow hunger death. The right of a woman, forced to undergo an abortion due to lack of alternatives, to have an alternative. Because it is a lie that present day women can make their own choices. If a woman has only one option, which is to abort, there is neither female freedom nor female self-determination.

So you see, I am here to defend women, to defend families, to require all those basic rights we already presented in parliament. Brothers of Italy is the party that proposed children income, which we believe more than citizenship income. I say this sincerely. Resources for those who give birth to a child, because those who bring a child into the world do a favor to society. [...]. We have asked for a moratorium in the UN to declare the uterus for rent as a universal crime, because that is truly violence against women. We want to introduce this theme in Europe, because it is outrageous that Europe considers birth at the same level as separation of house garbage. Low birth rate is the biggest open wound in Europe. If we do not face this, all the rest of what we do is useless. So why, if the European Union has an Erasmus program for mobility, if it has a Horizon program for scientific research, it cannot have a "Family" program to favor the birth rate? These are the kind of proposals we advance. Do they seem so crazy to you? Do they seem so obscurantist to you? Do you really think we want to make an end to female rights?

The middle Ages! But then, I mean, on closer inspection, the Middle Ages would also be the era of cathedrals and abbeys, the era in which the communes were born, the universities, the parliament, the era of Dante, Petrarca, Boccaccio, the age of St. Francis and St. Benedict. [...]

They attacked us on a personal level. "Shame on you! You talk about a natural family founded on marriage and yet you have a child born out of wedlock!" For that matter, I do plea for large families, yet I have but one child. Paradoxically, when they accuse me, they reinforce my stand. It simply demonstrates that what I try to achieve I do not do for my own interests. I fight for the good of Italian society. I believe the state should encourage marriage. I do not pretend the state should bestow on me those very privileges I require it to bestow on married families. That is my point. I believe in a society in which every choice has its consequences in terms of responsibility. I reject a society in which every desire or whim is a right. It's wrong!

I do not have a religious approach to this subject, even though I believe in God. I deliver my battles out of mere common sense. I am a person accustomed to asking myself questions, even uncomfortable ones, even profound ones. When I ask myself those questions I want credible answers. For sure, the high priests of left-dogmatic thought have not even tried to give sensible answers. And I can list dozens of these questions. The high priests defend a society that spends all its resources on immediate satisfaction. Is this normal? Can you call it "civilization"? Is it right that, while a newborn puppy dog may under no circumstance be torn out of its mother's womb, this can be done to a human child?

Italian judges deny parental authority to a heterosexual, married couple, because their dogmatic verdict promulgates that these two people are too old -in their fifty's- to raise their daughter. On the other hand, two gays in their fifties are allowed to buy a child abroad.

Why? Because, if they told us that Luana Englaro's father had to be free to pull the plug that kept his daughter alive, because no one knows better than a parent what is good for his child, why didn't the same rights apply to the parents of Charlie Gard, for those of Alfie Evans?

Why does death always win? Why is the sick life of Alfie Evans called futile? How much time before the life of a disabled person, or an elderly person, or anyone who does not match the canons of a perfect consumer, is considered useless? How much must it pass? And why do we focus on all kinds of discrimination, while pretending not to the globally concerted genocide of Christians?

I could ask many more of these questions. Why is the family an enemy? Why is family such a danger? There is but one answer to these questions: because the family defines us, because it is our identity. Because everything that defines us at this time is an enemy for those who would like us to no longer have an identity and that we were only slaves. Indeed, national identity is under attack, too, as is religious identity, and gender identity. I may not call myself "Italian", nor "Christian", nor "woman", nor "mother". I am supposed to be a mere number.

A number has no identity, no roots. It is the perfect slave at the mercy of great financial speculation. And this is the reason why today everybody is so scared. However, we do not want to be numbers, *we are here to say that we are not numbers,* we will defend the value of the human person, of every single human person, because each of us has a unique and unrepeatable genetic code. And this, like it or not, is the consequence of something sacred, of something supernatural. We will defend it. We will defend God, our Fatherland and its families. We will do it in order to defend our freedom, because we categorically refuse to be treated like slaves at the mercy of financial speculation.

This is our mission, that is the one and only reason I came to Verona today. Chesterton wrote, more than a century ago: "Fires will be stirred up to show that two plus two is four. Swords will be drawn to show that leaves are green in summer".

That time has come, dear ladies and gentlemen.

EPILOGUE

What is to be done?

Given the evolutionary (chapter 1), historical (chapter 2), political (chapter 3), moral (chapter 4), and hard-working parental (chapter 5) contributions to the nature of a woman, on one hand, and her discriminatorily lower status than man's, on the other, the million-dollar question is how to work for a more just future.

The answer has been given in chapter 3, and consists in my pen name: Niccolò di Bernardo dei Machiavelli, the father of that immoral political game that in many foreign languages is called "Machiavellism".

Of course I am not encouraging anybody (man nor woman) to act immorally, but only to study the relation between a political measure and its social consequences.

For example, organizing big manifestations against women's discrimination is about the worst decisions a women's-rights-platform could ever take. Why? Just read

Machiavelli's book "Il Principe" ("the prince", or more generally, "the guy in power"). Another example of an extremely counterproductive measure is encouraging abortions. For E-wired brains this is quite difficult to capture, so, my dear women, focus on your S-wired brain part. *Abortion is a mere gain only for men*, (i) because they obtain sex for free, without ABBA "affairs" (take a chance on me) or other forms of parental bonding, and (ii) because they are the moguls inverting in the abortion industry.

Obviously, the more S-wired women rebuke: "OK, but free sex is a right for us, too, is it not?" The actual answer is a moral negative. Nobody has the "right" to free sex, neither women nor men. Those who mean so, and usurp of a non-existing right, not only harm the female environment, but also end up in addictive misery. Unlike smoking cigarettes or using mentally debilitating drugs, which have their negative side-effects, like lung cancer and brain degradation (both not curable), sex-addiction has less life-shortening consequences. It is like if smoking cigarettes had no medical consequences at all, and cigarettes were sold at very low prices. In this case, everybody would be addicted to cigarettes. The same holds for sex: the pleasure lasts more or less one cigarette's smoking time. Moreover, the more frequently one has sex, the less exciting it becomes. Inevitably sex addiction leads to a sad, isolated life, due to the individual's plunge in full egotism.

Dear materialist, however sure you might think that God is the drug for the weak, 2000 years of medical research still did not result in a single attempt for an anti-sadness medical drug without side effects. Not even in the alternative circuits, where it is more than known that disco-drugs make one happy only by losing mental control. So, my dear S-wired women, is your proposal along one the above materialistic lines? Or do you finally give up, and acknowledge that happiness has but a single cause, and a spiritual one at that: having done moral good.

For the here mentioned reasons my proposal is to found a political party pressing for a just treatment of E-wired women: An E-wired women's party. As mentioned in chapter 3, your main goal is to achieve righteous financial retributions for your labor spent on raising future tax-payers with a psychologically balanced personality. This should be obvious to all E-wired women.

The rules are clear, but only comprehensible to S-wired brains: (i) the higher graduations your children obtain while going to school, the higher your salaries, and (ii) the more taxes your children pay, the higher your pension.

Believe me, the endless fight between democrats and republicans is nothing but a cover-up for the deep state. As long as ordinary, righteous US citizens keep focused on this opposition, nobody goes sniffing for a deep state mafia. Hence whenever republicans and democrats tend to find each other regarding a specific political matter, that very mafia will do anything to explode that fraternization. The only thing that is able to bring EZ (US' deep state and Rothschild's mafia) down, is a fraternized American population.

Nobody can doubt that S-wired goals are useless. It suffices to look at some three centuries of US history. For women it only brought the female voting right, passive and active. That is about it.

And how is my E-wired proposal going to help S-wired women, with S-wired ambitions, like having no kids and spending all your life for climbing the business or political ladder? Well, you of all women should understand this best, with your S-wired brains. When E-wired women receive a righteous salary, they will stick to the less appreciated part-time jobs, and be no competence for you. Moreover, the male respect for S-wired women will rise strongly, as the few women available on the S-market are on average better professionals than men, who all compete, indiscriminately and independently of their brain wiring, for the same S-job. Summarizing, even though the political E-party only aims at ensuring righteous salaries and pensions for E-wired women, the social appreciation of S-wired women will rise together with the E-political success.

And what is in this E-party plan for non-conventional women, like LGTB and whatever other wonderful variations (including seekers of controlled animal penetration)? Personally, I believe your life is a moral lie. That is nothing but the conviction of an old resentful S-wired male, of course. However, I do regard other people's freedom much higher than my conservative idée-fixes. So let me ask the LGTB community one simple question. In what society will you have more hope of being accepted as free citizens: In a society in which the majority of women have an equal social status to the majority of men, or in a society in which the majority of women is treated disrespectfully by men? Hence, I propose you find some way for fighting for your rights *without disrespect for women who choose traditional options.*

With my limited, S-wired brains, I can only conceive that all *rational women*, whatever their brain-wiring or sexual orientation, will vote for your E-party. That is a potential maximum of half the US population. It might even put a definitive end to the two-party system that tears up the thoroughly manipulated US society since uncountable generations.

www.ingramcontent.com/pod-product-compliance
Lightning Source LLC
Chambersburg PA
CBHW050736030426
42336CB00012B/1594